Sustainability at the Cutting Edge

Sustainability at the Cutting Edge

Emerging technologies for low energy buildings

Second edition

Peter F. Smith

AMSTERDAM • BOSTON • HEIDELBERG • LONDON • NEW YORK • OXFORD
PARIS • SAN DIEGO • SAN FRANCISCO • SINGAPORE • SYDNEY • TOKYO
Architectural Press is an imprint of Elsevier

ELSEVIER

Architectural
Press

Architectural Press
An imprint of Elsevier
Linacre House, Jordan Hill, Oxford OX2 8DP, UK
30 Corporate Drive, Suite 400, Burlington, MA 01803, USA

First edition 2003
Second edition 2007

Notice
No responsibility is assumed by the publisher for any injury and/or damage
to persons or property as a matter of products liability, negligence or
otherwise, or from any use or operation of any methods, products,
instructions or ideas contained in the material herein. Because of rapid
advances in the medical sciences, in particular, independent verification
of diagnoses and drug dosages should be made

British Library Cataloguing in Publication Data
Smith, Peter F. (Peter Frederick), 1930–
    Sustainability at the cutting edge: emerging technologies
    for low energy buildings. —2nd ed.
    1.   Architecture and energy conservation   2.   Architecture–
    Environmental aspects
    I. Title
    720.4'72

Library of Congress Cataloging-in-Publication Data
A catalog record for this book is available from the Library of Congress

ISBN-13: 978-0-7506-8300-5
ISBN-10: 0-7506-8300-7

For information on all Architectural Press publications
visit our website at www.architecturalpress.com

Typeset by Charon Tec Ltd (A Macmillan Company), Chennai, India
www.charontec.com
Printed and bound in Italy

07 08 09 10 11   11 10 9 8 7 6 5 4 3 2 1

Contents

Foreword

With mounting anxieties about climate change and the long-term outlook for energy, the role of renewable energy is becoming ever more critical. This book responds to these concerns by examining technologies ranging from microgeneration of power for individual homes to multi-megawatt technologies for base-load electricity. This second, enlarged edition reviews the latest advances in the technologies, as well as adding new case studies.

As the century progresses, the world will increasingly be subject to stress from global warming, an increasing population and the explosive economic growth of some developing countries. The social and economic survival of the planet will ultimately depend on the capacity of carbon neutral energy systems to replace reliance on fossil fuels. This book is a pointer to the technologies that will be able to help meet these changing requirements.

Lord Rogers of Riverside
Founder of the Richard Rogers Partnership

Introduction

In October 2001 the Royal Institute of British Architects hosted a conference on the subject of *Sustainability at the Cutting Edge*, which inspired the title of this book. The opening address was delivered by Sir John Houghton, a world authority on climate change issues. The aim of the conference was to provide an overview of the science and technology behind sources of renewable energy which would assume prominence in the next decade. This review was placed in the context of increasing concern about the impact of climate change and the fact that the built environment in countries like the UK is the worst culprit in terms of carbon dioxide emissions.

What has changed since the first edition was published in 2003?

Scientists are being continually surprised at the rate at which global-warming-related events are happening. Arctic and Antarctic ice sheets are melting faster than ever, as are mountain glaciers; permafrost is melting with dire consequences for buildings and roads; hurricanes in the 4 and 5 category are occurring with increasing frequency. Predictions of the impact of global warming on long-term temperatures are being regularly upgraded.

There is now a widespread acceptance of the human responsibility for most of the global warming. Even the White House accepts the science but still does not agree with most nations as to the solution. On the other hand, with Russia coming on board, the Kyoto Protocol was finally ratified. Unfortunately it is evident that very few signatories are on course to meet their obligations.

A UK government report of March 2006 gives an indication of the role of CO_2 in forcing global warming over the next 100 years if current emission levels are not curbed. Emissions are continuing to rise, even in the UK, despite its ambitious abatement targets. The economies of China and India are growing at 9% and 7% per year respectively. Most of that expansion is generated by fossil fuels, predominantly coal. Figure 1 indicates the contribution to global warming up to 2100 of current greenhouse gases relative to CO_2. Each greenhouse gas has a different capacity to cause warming depending on its radiative properties, molecular weight and life within the atmosphere.

The second Iraq war has introduced a huge uncertainty factor into security of oil supplies since the Middle East boasts the main concentration of reserves. The monopoly of gas supplies by Russia led to serious supply problems for neighbouring Ukraine in 2005, which had repercussions across much of Europe. Towards the end of 2005 the oil price exceeded a record $70 a barrel with a prediction that it will exceed $100 a barrel within a year. Wholesale gas price rose 60% in a year. These events are changing the climate of opinion as regards renewables.

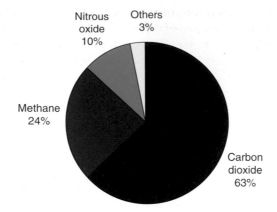

Global Warming Potentials for selected gases from the IPCC Third Assessment Report

Figure 1   Relative contributions to global warming over the next 100 years of current greenhouse gases according to DEFRA

On a world scale there is increasing investment in research and development of clean energy technologies with a number of major advances since the 2003 edition. At the same time, some of the technologies which were on the margins are now moving into the mainstream.

Soon we should see the next generation of PVs on the market, probably based on nanotechnology which will be significantly cheaper than silicon-based cells. Already in Germany and Japan economies of scale are being realized, thanks to government support. By, say, 2020, here millions of homes and offices could be pocket power stations feeding the grid or creating hydrogen for fuel cells. The UK government is coming round to acknowledging this in its 2006 report on a new microgeneration programme called 'Our Energy Strategy – power from the people'. This includes microfuel cells.

Buildings are likely to play a major role in a future energy scenario. They can be daytime power stations through photovoltaic cells (PVs) on roofs and elevations and microcombined heat and power. The Energy Saving Trust argues that 30–40% of the UK's electricity could come from home installations by 2050. At the moment PVs are not cost-effective set against conventional fossil generation. But things are changing as fossil fuel security becomes questionable. So, not only should we factor-in the climate change benefit but also the security gain. Quantify these and offset them against the cost and PVs will soon be a viable proposition.

Fuel cell technology is where another major breakthrough should occur. Many analysts believe that fuel cells will be the prime energy source in the future both for buildings and for transport. Their fuel is hydrogen and oxygen from the air and their products: water, heat and electricity. Being modular, they can be scaled to meet almost any requirement, from an individual home to a grid-connected power plant. For the next two decades or so static fuel cells will get their hydrogen from reformed natural gas. By 2050 experts predict we will have fully embraced the hydrogen economy. Making hydrogen will be the principal energy-related industry. Mark this quote from the President of Texaco Technology Ventures, from an address to the US House of Representatives Science Committee:

Market forces, greenery, and innovation are shaping the future of our industry and propelling us inexorably towards hydrogen energy. Those who don't pursue it . . . will rue it.

The dream of high-energy physics is commercial nuclear fusion, said to be appreciably safer than fission and not nearly so productive of waste. Now that massive international research funding is being directed towards it, mostly to a huge facility in Japan, there is growing confidence that it will be market-ready by the middle of the century.

As regards high energy density renewables, the UK is almost uniquely favoured with some of the strongest tidal currents and range of rise and fall in the world. A few demonstration projects are in place which should inspire even the most cautious government that there are reliable and tested technologies that can produce predictable electricity up to gigawatt scale from the marine environment.

In the UK energy policy is focused on wind power to deliver its CO_2 abatement targets up to 2020. However, since 2003 there has been increasing uncertainty about the capacity of wind to perform to expectations. For example, James Lovelock[1] quotes Niels Gram of the Danish Federation of Industries: 'Many of us thought that wind was the 100% solution for the future but we were wrong. In fact, taking all energy needs into account, it is only a 3% solution.' Lovelock also cites evidence from Germany that wind energy was available only 16% of the time. Based on his calculations, to supply the UK's present electricity needs would require 138,000 2 MW machines at three to the square mile thus covering an area larger than Wales. Despite the voices of caution the UK is going ahead with vast new offshore wind farms, notably the 270 unit 1000 MW installation off the Kent coast.

There is also a professional view that the most unpredictable power which the grid could accommodate without becoming destabilized is 10 GW.[2] Alongside these supply initiatives it is essential that we look seriously at demand-side reductions. There is no excuse now not to embrace superinsulation standards for domestic buildings. It's time we abandoned our superstitious attachment to cavity walls. On the continent they have no problem with this.

In commercial buildings the main energy cost is often electricity, mostly for lighting. This is set to change dramatically with the development of light-emitting diodes (LEDs) producing white light. An LED around 1–2 cm will emit the equivalent of a 60 W bulb using only 3 W. It will have a life expectancy of 100,000 hours.

Developments in optical fibre technology will also reduce energy demand in the commercial sector. The photonic revolution is almost upon us, and will be fully realized when the barriers to photonic switching are overcome. Then the all-photonic computer will use much less power and generate almost no heat.

There is no doubt that information technology will progress at an exponential rate. Photonic materials will play a major part in this revolution. The vision is for the whole world to be linked to an optical fibre superhighway based on photonic materials. The same must be said of nanotechnology, which is already leading developments in next generation photovoltaic cells.[3]

In March 2006 the UK government admitted that it was not going to achieve its target of a 20% reduction in CO_2 emissions by 2010. Ironically, this coincided with the fact that in April 2006 a private member's bill, The Climate Change and Sustainable Energy Bill, received the Royal Assent and, in the same month, new Building Regulations Part L (conservation of fuel and power) came into force. These are framed in such a way as to make buildings be considered holistically rather than element by element. This is a significant departure which will encourage architects and designers to work as a team from the outset of a project. It will also favour designers who are versatile with 3D modelling software since there is a 'simplified building energy model' (SBEM) with software which aims to make the design process easier.

The first edition began with a transcript of the keynote lecture presented by Sir John Houghton at the RIBA conference that inspired this book. For the second edition he has kindly agreed to replace this with his Prince Philip Lecture delivered at the Royal Society of Arts in May 2005 entitled *Climate change and sustainable energy*. It would be impossible to find a more appropriate introduction to the new edition.

Peter F. Smith

Notes

1. James Lovelock (2006), *The revenge of Gaia*, Penguin/Allen Lane, p. 83
2. 'Why UK wind power should not exceed 10 GW, Hugh Sharman, *Civil Engineering* 158, November 2005, pp. 161–69

For more information on the ecological role of buildings see *Architecture in a Climate of Change*, 2nd edition, 2005 and *Eco-refurbishment – a guide to saving and producing energy in the home*, 2004, both Peter F. Smith and Architectural Press.

Acknowledgements

I am indebted to the researchers and construction professionals who readily gave permission for the inclusion of their work in the text. These include Dr Koen Steemers of Cambridge Architectural Research, Arup Associates for BedZED diagrams, Christopher John Hancock for the images of Malmö, Jeremy Stacy Architects for the Council Offices, King's Lynn, Fielden Clegg Bradley for the National Trust Offices, Swindon, XCO$_2$ for the triple helix wind generator image and Pilkington plc for the image of Herne Sodingen government training centre. I also owe my thanks to Dr Randall Thomas of Max Fordham and Partners and Robin Saunders of the Department of Mechanical Engineering, Sheffield University for reviewing the manuscript and giving me the benefit of their expertise in the sphere of renewable energy. I must also record my thanks to my wife Jeannette for her sterling work in making up for my deficiencies in proofreading. Finally, my special thanks are due to Sir John Houghton for allowing me to begin the book with his Prince Philip Lecture at the Royal Society of Arts in 2005 and to Lord Rogers of Riverside for his continued support.

1 Climate change and sustainable energy: The 2005 Prince Philip Lecture at the Royal Society of Arts by Sir John Houghton CBE FRS

Your Royal Highness, it is a pleasure and privilege to be presenting your lecture this evening. You have been a great supporter of sustainability. In particular, you are pursuing some highly innovative sustainable energy projects at Windsor Castle that provide marvellous examples of the variety of ways forward for us in the energy field.

There is a fine exhibition in the Tate Gallery at the moment of works by Turner, Whistler and Monet. A hundred years ago, Monet spent time in London and painted wonderful pictures of the light coming through the smog. London was blighted by *local pollution* from domestic and industrial chimneys around the city itself. Thanks to the Clean Air Acts beginning in the 1950s, those awful smogs belong to the past, although London's atmosphere could be still cleaner.

But what I am talking about today is *global pollution* – emissions of gases such as carbon dioxide to which we are all contributing, that spread around the whole atmosphere and affect everybody. Global pollution requires global solutions.

Let me start with a quick summary of some of the science of global warming. By absorbing infrared or 'heat' radiation from the Earth's surface, 'greenhouse gases' present in the atmosphere – such as water vapour and carbon dioxide – act as blankets over the Earth, keeping it warmer than it would otherwise be. The existence of this natural 'greenhouse effect' has been known for nearly two hundred years; it is essential to the provision of our current climate, to which ecosystems and we humans have adapted.

Since the beginning of the Industrial Revolution around 1750, one of these greenhouse gases – carbon dioxide – has increased by more than 30% and is now at a higher concentration in the atmosphere than it has been for many thousands of years (Fig. 1.1). Chemical analysis demonstrates that this increase is largely due to the burning of the fossil fuels coal, oil and gas. If no action is taken to curb these emissions, the carbon dioxide concentration will rise during the twenty-first century to two or three times its preindustrial level.

The climate record over the last 1,000 years (Fig. 1.2) shows a lot of natural variability, including, for instance, the 'medieval warm period' and the 'little ice age'. The rise in global

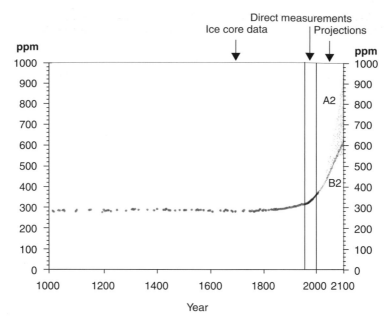

Figure 1.1   Concentration of carbon dioxide in the atmosphere from 1000 AD and projected to 2100 under typical IPCC scenarios

average temperature (and its rate of rise) during the twentieth century is well outside the range of known natural variability. The year 1998 is the warmest in the instrumental record. A more striking statistic is that each of the first 8 months of 1998 was the warmest on record for that month. There is strong evidence that most of the warming over the last 50 years is due to the increase of greenhouse gases, especially carbon dioxide. Confirmation of this is also provided by observations of the warming of the oceans. The period of 'global dimming' from about 1950 to 1970 is most likely due to the increase in atmospheric particles (especially sulphates) from industrial sources. These particles reflect sunlight, hence tending to cool the surface and mask some of the warming effect of greenhouse gases.

Over the twenty-first century the global average temperature is projected to rise by between 2 and 6°C (3.5 to 11°F) from its preindustrial level – the range represents different assumptions about emissions of greenhouse gases and the sensitivity of the climate model used in making the estimate (Fig. 1.2). For *global average* temperature, a rise of this amount is large. Its difference between the middle of an ice age and the warm periods in between is only about 5 or 6°C (9 to 11°F). So, associated with likely warming in the twenty-first century will be a rate of change of climate equivalent to, say, half an ice age in less than 100 years – a larger rate of change than for at least 10,000 years. Adapting to this will be difficult for humans and many ecosystems.

Talking in terms of changes of global average temperature, however, tells us rather little about the impacts of global warming on human communities. Some of the most obvious impacts will be due to the rise in sea level that occurs because ocean water expands as it is heated. The projected rise is of the order of half a metre (20 inches) a century and will continue for many centuries – to warm the deep oceans as well as the surface waters takes a long time. This will cause large problems for human communities living in low lying regions. Many areas – for instance Bangladesh (where about 10 million live within the one metre contour – Fig. 1.3), southern China, islands in the Indian and Pacific oceans and similar places elsewhere in the world – will be impossible to protect and many millions of people will be displaced.

Variations of the Earth's surface temperature: 1000 to 2100
1000 to 1861, N. Hemisphere, proxy data; 1861 to 2000 Global, instrumental;
2000 to 2100, SRES projections

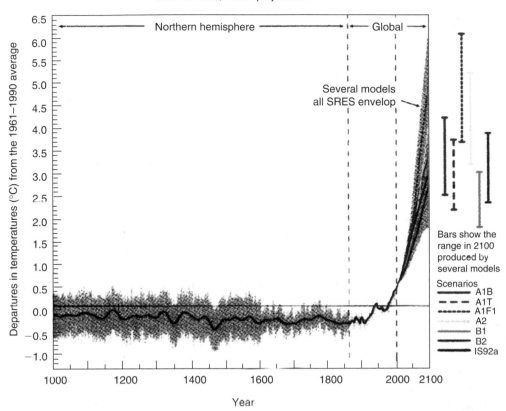

Figure 1.2 Variations of the average near-surface air temperature: 1000–1861, N Hemisphere from proxy data; 1861–2000, global instrumental; 2000–2100, under a range of IPCC projections with further shading to indicate scientific uncertainty

There will also be impacts from extreme events. The extremely unusual high temperatures in central Europe during the summer of 2003 led to the deaths of more than 20,000 people. Careful analysis leads to the projection that such summers are likely to be average by the middle of the twenty-first century and cool by the year 2100.

Water is becoming an increasingly important resource. A warmer world will lead to more evaporation of water from the surface, more water vapour in the atmosphere and more precipitation on average. Of greater importance is the fact that the increased condensation of water vapour in cloud formation leads to increased latent heat of condensation being released. Since this latent heat release is the largest source of energy driving the atmosphere's circulation, the hydrological cycle will become more intense. This means a tendency to more intense rainfall events and also less rainfall in some semi-arid areas. Since, on average, floods and droughts are the most damaging of the world's disasters (see Table 1.1), their greater frequency and intensity is bad news for most human communities, and especially for those regions such as south east Asia and sub-Saharan Africa where such events already occur all too frequently. It is these sorts of events that provide some credence to the comparison of climate with weapons of mass destruction.

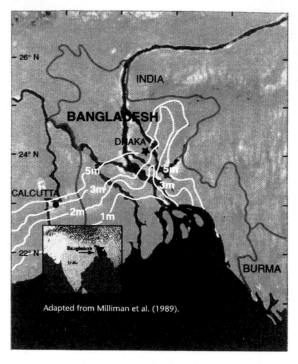

Figure 1.3   Land affected in Bangladesh by various amounts of sea-level rise

Table 1.1   Major floods in the 1990s

1991, 1994–5, 1998 – China; average disaster cost, 1989–96, 4% of GDP
1993 – Mississippi & Missouri, USA; flooded area equal to one of great lakes
1997 – Europe; 162,000 evacuated and >$5bn loss
1998 – Hurricane Mitch in central America; 9,000 deaths, economic loss in Honduras & Nicaragua, 70% and 45% of GDP
1999 – Venezuela; flooding led to landslide, 30,000 deaths
2000–1 – Mozambique; two floods left more than half a million homeless

Sea-level rise, changes in water availability and extreme events will lead to increasing pressure from environmental refugees. A careful estimate has suggested that, due to climate change, there could be more than 150 million extra refugees by 2050.

In addition to the main impacts summarized above are changes about which there is less certainty but which, if they occurred, would be highly damaging and possibly irreversible. For instance, large changes are being observed in polar regions. If the temperature rises more than about 3°C (~5°F) in the area of Greenland, it is estimated that meltdown of the ice cap would begin. Complete meltdown is likely to take 1,000 years or more but it would add 7 metres (23 feet) to the sea level.

A further concern is regarding the thermo-haline circulation (THC) – a circulation in the deep oceans, partially sourced from water that has moved in the Gulf Stream from the tropics to the region between Greenland and Scandinavia. Because of evaporation on the way, the water is not only cold, but salty, and hence of higher density than the surrounding water. It therefore tends to sink and provides the source for a slow circulation at low levels that connects all the oceans together. This sinking assists in maintaining the Gulf Stream itself. In a globally warmed world, increased precipitation together with fresh water from melting ice will decrease the water's salinity, making it less likely to sink. The circulation will therefore weaken and possibly even cut off, leading to large regional changes of climate. Evidence from paleoclimate history shows that such cut-off has occurred at times in the past. It is such an event that is behind the highly speculative happenings in the film *The Day After Tomorrow.*

I have spoken so far about adverse impacts. You will ask: 'are none of the impacts positive?' There are some positive impacts. For instance, in Siberia and other areas at high northern latitudes, winters will be less cold and growing seasons will be longer. Also, increased concentrations of carbon dioxide have a fertilizing effect on some plants and crops which, providing there are adequate supplies of water and nutrients, will lead to increased crop yields in some places, probably most notably in northern mid-latitudes. However, careful studies demonstrate that adverse impacts will far outweigh positive effects; more so as temperatures rise more than 1 or 2°C (2 to 3.5°F) above preindustrial.

Many people ask how sure we are about the scientific story I have just presented. Let me explain that it is based very largely on the extremely thorough work of the Intergovernmental Panel on Climate Change (IPCC) and its last major report published in 2001. The scientific literature on climate change has increased enormously over the last decade. The basic science of anthropogenic climate change has been confirmed. The main uncertainties lie in our knowledge of feedbacks in the climate system, especially those associated with the effects of clouds. Recent research has tended to indicate increased likelihood of the more damaging impacts.

The Intergovernmental Panel on Climate Change (IPCC)

The IPCC was formed in 1988 jointly by the World Meteorological Organization and the United Nations Environment Programme. I had the privilege of being chairman or co-chairman of the Panel's scientific assessment from 1988 to 2002. Hundreds of scientists drawn from many countries were involved as contributors and reviewers in these assessments. Our task was honestly and objectively to distinguish what is reasonably well known and understood from those areas with large uncertainty. The IPCC has produced three assessments – in 1990, 1995 and 2001 – covering science, impacts and analyses of policy options. The IPCC 2001 report is in four volumes, each of about 1,000 pages and containing many thousands of references to the scientific literature. Because the IPCC is an intergovernmental body, the reports' Summaries for Policymakers were agreed sentence by sentence by meetings of governmental delegates from about 100 countries – including all the world's major countries. No assessment on any other scientific topic has been so thoroughly researched and reviewed.

The work of the IPCC is backed by the world-wide scientific community. A joint statement of support was issued in May 2001 by the national science academies of Australia, Belgium, Brazil, Canada, the Caribbean, China, France, Germany, India, Indonesia, Ireland, Italy, Malaysia, New Zealand, Sweden and the UK. It stated: 'We recognise the IPCC as the world's most reliable source of information on climate change and its causes, and we endorse its method of achieving consensus.' In 2001, a report of the United States National Academy of Sciences commissioned by the President George W Bush administration also supported the IPCC's conclusions.

Unfortunately, there are strong vested interests that have spent tens of millions of dollars on spreading misinformation about the climate change issue. First they tried to deny the existence of any scientific evidence for rapid climate change due to human activities. More recently they have largely accepted the fact of anthropogenic climate change but argue that its impacts will not be great, that we can 'wait and see' and, in any case, we can always 'fix' the problem if it turns out to be substantial. The scientific evidence cannot support such arguments.

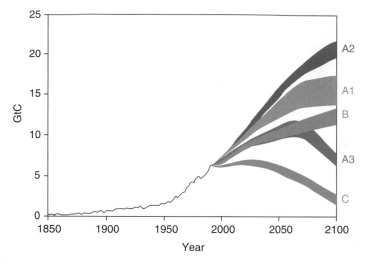

Figure 1.4   Global emissions of carbon dioxide from fossil fuel burning (in billions of tonnes of carbon) up to 1990 and as projected to 2100 under World Energy Council scenarios, As and Bs with various 'business as usual assumptions' and C for 'ecologically driven scenario' that would lead to stabilization of carbon dioxide concentration at about 500 ppm

Because of the work of the IPCC and its first report in 1990, the Earth Summit at Rio de Janeiro in 1992 could address the climate change issue and the action that needed to be taken. The Framework Convention on Climate Change (FCCC) – agreed by more than 160 countries, signed by President George Bush for the USA and subsequently ratified unanimously by the US Senate – agreed that Parties to the Convention should take 'precautionary measures to anticipate, prevent or minimise the causes of climate change and mitigate its adverse effects. Where there are threats of irreversible damage, lack of full scientific certainty should not be used as a reason for postponing such measures'.

More particularly, the Objective of the FCCC in its Article 2 is 'to stabilise greenhouse gas concentrations in the atmosphere at a level that does not cause dangerous interference with the climate system' and that is consistent with sustainable development. Such stabilization would also eventually stop further climate change. However, because of the long time that carbon dioxide resides in the atmosphere, the lag in the response of the climate to changes in greenhouse gases (largely because of the time taken for the ocean to warm), and the time taken for appropriate human action to be agreed, the achievement of such stabilization will take at least the best part of a century.

Global emissions of carbon dioxide to the atmosphere from fossil fuel burning are currently approaching 7 billion tonnes of carbon per annum and rising rapidly (Fig. 1.4). Unless strong measures are taken, they will reach two or three times their present levels during the twenty-first century and stabilization of greenhouse gas concentrations or of climate will be nowhere in sight. To stabilize carbon dioxide concentrations, emissions during the twenty-first century must reduce to a fraction of their present levels before the century's end.

The reductions in emissions must be made globally; all nations must take part. However, there are very large differences between greenhouse gas emissions in different countries. Expressed in tonnes of carbon per capita per annum, they vary from about 5.5 for the USA, 2.2 for Europe, 0.7 for China and 0.2 for India (Fig. 1.5). Ways need to be found to achieve reductions that are realistic and equitable – for instance, by following a suggestion of the Global Commons Institute called Contraction and Convergence that proposes convergence

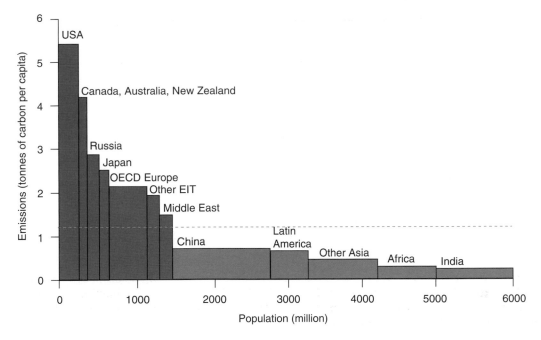

Figure 1.5   Carbon dioxide emissions in 2000 per capita for different countries and groups of countries

within a few decades to equal per capita allowances of carbon dioxide together with trading within those allowances.

The Kyoto Protocol set up by the FCCC represents a beginning for the process of reduction, averaging about 5% below 1990 levels by 2012 by those developed countries which have ratified the protocol. It is an important start, demonstrating the achievement of a useful measure of international agreement on such a complex issue. It also introduces, for the first time, international trading of greenhouse gas emissions so that reductions can be achieved in the most cost-effective ways.

Serious discussion is now beginning about international agreements for emissions reductions post Kyoto. These must include all major emitters in developed and developing countries. On what eventual level of stabilization of carbon dioxide, for instance, should these negotiations focus? To stop damaging climate change, the level needs to be as low as possible. In the light of the FCCC Objective it must also allow for sustainable development. Let me give two examples of stabilization proposals. In 1996 the European Commission proposed a limit for the rise in global average temperature from its preindustrial value of 2°C, which implies a stabilization level for carbon dioxide of about 430 ppm (allowing for the effect of other greenhouse gases at their 1990 levels). The second example comes from Lord John Browne, Chief Executive Officer of British Petroleum – one of the world's largest oil companies – who, in a recent speech, proposed 'stabilization in the range 500–550 ppm' that 'with care could be achieved without disrupting economic growth'.

Let us consider carbon dioxide stabilization at 500 ppm. If the effect of other greenhouse gases at their 1990 levels is added, it is about equivalent to doubled carbon dioxide at its preindustrial level and a rise in global averaged temperature of about 2.5°C. Although climate change would eventually largely be halted – albeit not for well over a hundred years – the climate change impacts at such a level would be large. A steady rise in sea level will continue for many centuries, heatwaves such as in Europe in 2003 would be commonplace, devastating floods and droughts would be much more common in many places and Greenland would most likely start to melt down. The aim should be, therefore, to stabilize at a lower level. But is that possible?

In 2004, the International Energy Agency (IEA) published a *World Energy Outlook* that, in its words, 'paints a sobering picture of how the global energy system is likely to evolve from now to 2030'. With present governments' policies, the world's energy needs will be almost 60% higher in 2030 than they are now. Fossil fuels will dominate, meeting most of the increase in overall energy use. Energy-related emissions of carbon dioxide will grow marginally faster than energy use and will be more than 60% higher in 2030 than now (Reference Scenario, Fig. 1.6a). Over two-thirds of the projected increase in emissions will come from developing countries.

The *Outlook* also presents an alternative scenario which analyses the global impact of environmental and energy-security policies that countries around the world are already considering, as well as the effects of faster deployment of energy-efficient technologies. However, even in this scenario, global emissions in 2030 are substantially greater than they are today (Fig. 1.6b). Neither scenario comes close to creating the turnaround in the global profile required.

The UK Government has taken a lead on this issue and agreed a target for the reduction of greenhouse gas emissions of 60% by 2050 – predicated on a stabilization target of doubled carbon dioxide concentrations together with a recognition that developed countries will need to make greater reductions to allow some headroom for developing countries. Economists in the UK Government Treasury Department have estimated the cost to the UK economy of achieving this target. On the assumption of an average growth in the UK economy of 2.25% p.a., they estimated a cost of no more than the equivalent of 6 months' growth over the 50 year period. Similar costs for achieving stabilization have been estimated by the IPCC.

The effect of such a reduction – if agreed by all developed countries – is shown in Fig. 1.6c, together with a scenario for developing countries that increases by 1% p.a. until 2030, followed by level emissions to 2050. For this, the 500 ppm curve is approximately followed, but for developing countries to be satisfied with such a modest growth presents a very large challenge. Even more challenging for developed and developing countries would be the measures required to stabilize at 450 ppm (Fig. 1.6d).

Let me now address the actions that need to be taken if the larger reductions that I have argued for are to be achieved. Three sorts of actions are required. First, there is energy efficiency. Very approximately one third of energy is employed in buildings (domestic and commercial), one third in transport and one third by industry. Large savings can be made in all three sectors, many with significant savings in cost. But to achieve these savings in practice seems surprisingly difficult.

Take buildings, for example. Recent projects such as BedZED in south London demonstrate that 'zero energy' buildings are a practical possibility (ZED = Zero Energy Development). Initial costs are a little larger than for conventional buildings but the running costs a lot less, but most recent housing in Britain – built or planned – continues to be very unsatisfactory in terms of a level of energy sustainability that is easily achievable. Why, for instance, is combined heat and power (CHP) not the norm for new housing estates? Significant efficiency savings are also achievable in the transport sector. Within the industrial sector, some serious drives for energy savings are already becoming apparent. Eleven of the world's largest companies have already achieved savings in energy that have translated into money savings of US$5.5bn.

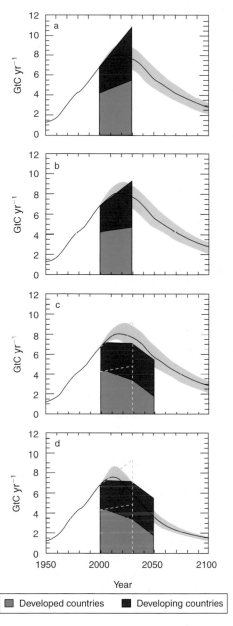

Emissions data from IEA World Energy Review 2004, stabilization curves from Met Office Hadley Centre

Figure 1.6   Carbon dioxide emissions from fossil fuel burning: from 1950–2000, actual emissions; from 2000 to 2100, profile of emissions leading to CO_2 stabilization at 500 ppm (a, b and c) and 450 ppm (d) – shaded area indicates uncertainty. Cyan and magenta areas show projected emissions from International Energy Agency scenarios. Reference Scenario (a), Alternative Scenario (b) for developed countries (cyan) and developing (magenta). (c) and (d) show Alternative Scenario in dotted lines, for further explanation see text.

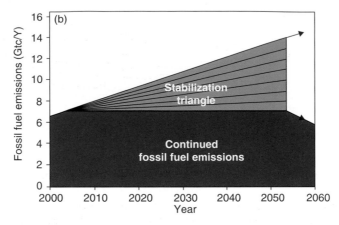

Figure 1.7   Fossil fuel dioxide emissions 2000–2060 showing growth reduced by seven stabilization 'wedges'

A simple presentation of the type of reductions that are required has been created by Professor Socolow of Princeton University. To counter the likely growth in global emissions of carbon dioxide from now until 2050, seven 'wedges' of reduction are proposed, each wedge amounting to 1 gigatonne of carbon per year in 2050 or 25 gigatonnes in the period up to 2050 (Fig. 1.7). Some of the possible 'wedges' he proposes are the following. They illustrate the scale of what is necessary.

- Buildings' efficiency – reduce emissions by 25%
- Vehicles' fuel use – from 30 to 60 mpg in 2bn vehicles
- Carbon capture and storage at 800 GW of coal plants
- Wind power from one million 2 MWp windmills
- Solar PV power from area of $(150\,km)^2$
- Nuclear power – 700 GW – 2 × current capacity
- Stop tropical deforestation and establish 300 Mha of new tree plantations
- Biofuel production (ethanol) from biomass on 250 Mha of land

---

Secondly, a wide variety of non-fossil fuel sources of energy are available for development and exploitation, such as biomass (including waste), solar power (both photovoltaic and thermal), hydro, wind, wave, tidal and geothermal energy. Thirdly, there are possibilities for sequestering carbon that would otherwise enter the atmosphere, either through the planting of forests or by pumping underground (for instance, in spent oil and gas wells). The opportunities for industry for innovation, development and investment in all these areas is large.

It is, of course, easy to present paper solutions (see example in box) but harder to see how they can be implemented. Questions are immediately raised, such as: 'what are the best options?' There is no one solution to the problem and no best technology. Further, different solutions will be appropriate in different countries or regions. Simplistic answers I have heard many times recently have been:

'*Leave it to the market that will provide in due course*' and '*The three solutions are Technology, Technology and Technology*'. The market and technology are essential and effective tools but poor masters. Solutions need to be much more carefully crafted than these tools can provide on their own. So how can the process start?

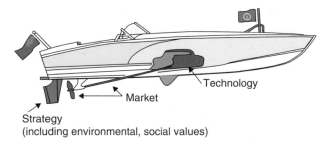

Technology

Market

Strategy
(including environmental, social values)

Figure 1.8   Where are we heading? – the need for an energy strategy. The boat flies national and UN flags to illustrate the need for national and international strategies

A long-term perspective is required. I like to think of it in terms of a voyage. For the boat we are taking, technology can be thought of as the engine and market forces as the propeller driven by the engine (Fig. 1.8). But where is the boat heading? Without a rudder and someone steering, the course will be arbitrary; it could even be disastrous. Every voyage needs a destination and a strategy to reach it. Let me mention four components of the strategy that should direct any solutions.

First the economy and environment must be addressed together. It has been said that 'the economy is a wholly owned subsidiary of the environment'. In a recent speech, Gordon Brown, the UK's Chancellor of the Exchequer, expanded on this idea when he said:

> *Environmental issues – including climate change – have traditionally been placed in a category separate from the economy and from economic policy. But this is no longer tenable. Across a range of environmental issues – from soil erosion to the depletion of marine stocks, from water scarcity to air pollution – it is clear now not just that economic activity is their cause, but that these problems in themselves threaten future economic activity and growth.*

Take the market. It responds overwhelmingly to price and the short term. It has been effective in bringing reduced energy prices over the last two decades. But in its raw form it takes no account of environmental or other external factors. Although there has been general agreement among economists for many years that such factors should be internalized in the market – for instance through carbon taxes or cap and trade arrangements – most governments have been slow to introduce such measures. An example where it is working comes from Norway, where the carbon tax that is levied makes it economic to pump carbon dioxide back into the strata from where gas is extracted. Aviation presents a contrary example where the absence of any economic measures is allowing global aviation to expand at a highly unsustainable rate.

Where are we heading? Components of energy strategy

- Market and technology are tools, not masters
- Long-term, not only short-term
- Economy and environment considered together – internalize external costs
- Get potential technologies to starting gate
- Address social and 'quality of life' values e.g. community benefits of local energy provision
- Energy security to be taken into account

Secondly, not all potential technologies are at the same stage of development. For good choices to be made, promising technologies need to be brought to the starting gate so that they can properly compete. This implies joint programmes between government and industry, the provision of adequate resources for research and development, the creation of demonstration projects and sufficient support to see technologies through to maturity. The market will provide rather little of this on its own. What are needed are appropriate incentive schemes. The UK Renewables Obligation scheme goes some way to providing what is required but is inadequate as it stands for bringing important technologies to the position where they can satisfactorily compete. For instance, the UK has some of the largest tides in the world. Energy from tidal streams, lagoons or barrages has the advantage over wind energy of being precisely predictable and of presenting few environmental or amenity problems. It has the potential of providing up to 20% of the UK's electricity at competitive prices. Given the right encouragement and incentives, there seems no technical reason why good demonstration projects cannot be established very soon so that some of this potential can be realized within the next decade – much earlier than the timing of 'beyond 2020' that is often mentioned for this technology to be brought in. Similar potential is available from wave energy to the north and west of Britain.

A third part of the strategy is to address the social and 'quality of life' implications arising from the way energy is provided to a community. For instance, energy coming from large central installations has very different knock-on social and community effects than that coming from small and local energy provision. The best urban solutions may be different from what is most appropriate in rural locations.

Addressing more than one problem at once is also part of this component of the strategy. For instance, it is not by accident that this lecture is listed under the drive to Zero Waste, which is one of the five Manifesto challenges of the Royal Society of Arts. Disposal of waste and generation of energy can frequently go together. There are many examples. I have already mentioned the BedZED development that obtains its heat and power from forestry residue. In Upper Austria, a population of 1.5 million obtains 14% of its total energy from local biomass projects including waste – this is planned to double by 2010. They benefit greatly from the community involvement such projects bring with them, illustrating another of the RSA Manifesto thrusts: that of 'fostering resilient communities that exercise creative stewardship'. The Energy Future Coalition in the USA is putting forward '25 by '25' – a target that 25% of total US energy needs should be provided from biomass sources by 2025. In contrast, the UK raises a mere 0.1% of its energy this way – one of the lowest levels in Europe. A report from the Royal Commission on Environmental Pollution has highlighted the barriers that are preventing development of energy from biomass and waste sources. The Commission believes that, provided the barriers are removed, these sources could provide 8% of total UK energy needs by 2050.

The Shell Foundation – of which I am a Trustee – is supporting the development of many biomass pilot schemes in poorer countries, ranging from using sewage from latrines in India, coconut shells in the Philippines and rice straw in China. All these could be multiplied many times over and point to an important component of the way forward for developing countries. Solar energy schemes can also be highly versatile in size or application. Small solar home systems (Fig. 1.9) can bring electricity in home-sized packages to villages in the third world – again with enormous benefits to local communities. At the other end of the size scale, large solar thermal or PV projects are being envisaged that couple electricity and hydrogen generation with desalination in desert regions where water is a scarce resource.

Fourthly, energy security must be part of the strategy and is increasingly being addressed by governments in many countries. How safe are gas pipelines crossing whole continents?

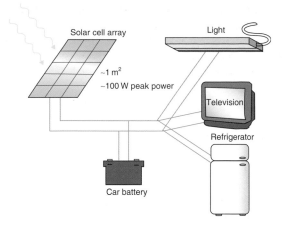

Figure 1.9 A simple 'solar home system' as is being marketed in many developing countries

How safe are nuclear power stations from terrorist attack or nuclear material from proliferation to terrorist groups? It is such considerations that put into question large expansion of the contribution from nuclear energy. However, there are hundreds of tonnes of plutonium now surplus from military programmes that could be used in nuclear power stations (and degraded in the process) assisting with greenhouse gas reductions in the medium term.

Diversity of source is clearly important. But thinking about security could be more integrated and holistic. Admiral Sir Julian Oswald, First Sea Lord more than ten years ago, suggested that defence policy and spending could be broadened to consider potential causes of conflict, such as the large scale damage and insecurity that increasingly will arise from climate change.

Let me now address those who argue that we can 'wait and see' before action is necessary. That is not a responsible position. The need for action is urgent for three reasons. The first reason is *scientific*. Because the oceans take time to warm, there is a lag in the response of climate to increasing greenhouse gases. Because of greenhouse gas emissions to date, a commitment to substantial change already exists, much of which will not be realized for 30 to 50 years. Further emissions just add to that commitment. The second reason is *economic*. Energy infrastructure, for instance in power stations, also lasts typically for 30 to 50 years. It is much more cost-effective to begin now to phase in the required infrastructure changes rather than having to make them much more rapidly later.

The third reason is *political*. Countries such as China and India are industrializing very rapidly. I heard a senior energy adviser to the Chinese Government speak recently. He said that China by itself would not be making big moves to non-fossil-fuel sources. When the developed nations of the west take action, they will take action – they will follow, not lead. China is building new electricity-generating capacity of about 1 GW power station every two weeks. If we want to provide an example of effective leadership, we need to start now.

Essential components of this leadership are, at the national level, that all parts of government should work in a joined-up way and that government and industry should together plan the necessary strategy. Internationally, European countries through the EU need to plan and act together, to work to bring the USA properly on board and to cooperate closely with developing countries so that they too can be part of the solution.

People often say to me that I am wasting my time talking about global warming. 'The world', they say, 'will never agree to take the necessary action'. I reply that I am optimistic for three reasons. First, I have experienced the commitment of the world scientific community (including scientists from many different nations, backgrounds and cultures) in painstakingly and honestly working together to understand the problems and assessing what needs to be done. Secondly, I believe the necessary technology is available for achieving satisfactory solutions. My third reason is that I believe we have a God-given task of being good stewards of creation. For our fulfilment as humans we need not just economic goals but moral and spiritual ones. Near the top of the list of such goals could be long-term care for our planet and its resources. Reaching out for such a goal could lead to nations and peoples working together more effectively and closely than is possible with many of the other goals on offer.

We, in the developed countries, have already benefited over many generations from abundant fossil fuel energy. The demands on our stewardship take on a special poignancy as we realize that the adverse impacts of climate change will fall disproportionately on poorer nations and tend to exacerbate the increasingly large divide between rich and poor.

My wife always reminds me when I speak on this subject that I need to indicate the sort of actions that individuals can take. There are some things that all of us can do. For instance, when purchasing vehicles or appliances we can choose ones that are fuel efficient; we can ensure our homes are as energy efficient as possible and buy our electricity from 'green' suppliers; we can use public transportation or car-share more frequently and we can support leaders in government or industry who are advocating or organizing the necessary solutions. To quote from Edmund Burke, a British parliamentarian of 200 years ago: 'No one made a greater mistake than he who did nothing because he could do so little.'

The UK has been a world leader on addressing climate change since 1988, the year in which Margaret Thatcher spoke about it in an address to the Royal Society. We are the first nation to set an emissions reduction target for 2050. This year, Prime Minister Tony Blair has put climate change at the top of his agenda for his presidency of the G8 and the EU. This is all good news. However, to many of us, Government seems to drag its feet. Matching action has failed to keep up with the fine words. In Europe, for instance, we are not leaders in renewable energy provision and many do not believe we will meet the targets for 2010 or 2020 that we have set for ourselves. To move the world forward we have to be seen to be moving ourselves. Both the challenge and the opportunity for the new UK Government are unmistakable.

Acknowledgements

I am grateful to Sir David King and John Ashton for valuable discussions regarding the topic of this lecture and to many colleagues in the Hadley Centre, especially Chris Jones and Fiona Smith, for helpful information and assistance with the lecture's preparation.

About the author

Sir John Houghton was co-chairman of the Scientific Assessment for the IPCC from 1988–2002. He was previously chairman of the Royal Commission on Environmental Pollution (1992–1998), Chief Executive of the Meteorological Office (1983–1991) and Professor of Atmospheric Physics, University of Oxford (1976–1983). He is currently chairman of the John Ray Initiative, a Trustee of the Shell Foundation and Honorary Scientist at the Hadley Centre.

2 Solar thermal power

So much for the evidence of climate change; now, what can be done? It is likely that solar thermal power will provide a major share of the renewable energy needed in the future since solar radiation is by far the largest potential renewable resource. About 1% of the earth's deserts covered with solar thermal plants would have supplied the world's total energy demand for the year 2000.

The solar thermal resource serves two energy domains – heat and electricity.

Solar heating

The United Nations Development Programme (UNDP) world energy assessment estimates the global use of energy to heat water to be 10,000 PJ.[1] This technology is especially important for rapidly growing cities like Mexico City and São Paulo which have a severe pollution problem as well as an energy problem.

There are two basic systems for solar heating:

- flat bed collectors
- vacuum tube collectors.

Flat bed collectors consist of metal plates coated matt black behind glass or plastic. They are tilted to maximize uptake of solar radiation. Behind the plates are pipes carrying the heat-absorbing medium, either water or air. Water for indirect systems contains antifreeze. The underside of the plates is insulated. Flat bed collectors realize temperatures around 35°C and are best employed to supply pre-heated water for a gas boiler or immersion heater.

It is increasingly becoming the case that the collector system incorporates a photovoltaic (PV) module to provide power for the circulating fan, making it a true zero fossil energy option.

Vacuum tube collectors

In this technology, evacuated tubes enclosed within an insulated steel casing work by exploiting the vacuum around the collector. This reduces the heat loss from the system, making them particularly suited to cooler climates like that experienced in the UK. They heat water to around 60°C but sometimes significantly higher. This means that domestic hot

Figure 2.1   Vacuum solar collectors on Professor Marmont's Farm, Nottinghamshire

water systems may have no need of additional heating. To realize their full potential they should be linked to a storage facility which stores excess warmth in summer to supplement winter heating (see Fig. 2.1).

Solar panels have traditionally been associated with providing domestic hot water (DHW). Solar water heaters comprise a solar collector array, an energy transfer system and a thermal storage unit. There are two basic principles involved:

- passive or thermosyphon systems in which circulation of the working fluid is driven by thermal buoyancy
- active solar whereby a heat transfer fluid is mechanically circulated through the collector.

There is a further division into direct or 'open loop' systems, in which potable water is circulated through the collectors, and 'closed loop' or indirect systems, which use an antifreeze heat transfer circulating fluid.

In thermosyphon systems the storage tank must be above the collectors. There are three configurations which can be directly connected to a horizontal tank:

- flat bed collectors
- parabolic trough collectors with the heat pipe absorber (see below) feeding directly into the base of the storage cylinder
- evacuated tube collectors.

This combined collector/storage system is limited to providing hot water during the day (see Figs 2.2–2.5).

Active solar systems can be open loop (Fig. 2.6) or closed loop, in which the circulating fluid passes through a coil heat exchanger within the storage tank (Fig. 2.7). This technology is being promoted by the International Energy Agency (IEA) via its solar heating and cooling programme. The IEA is an agency of the Organization for Economic Co-operation and Development (OECD). The potential for solar domestic hot water is about $1\,m^2$ per person.

Countries like those in the Middle East and China are exploiting this technology at an accelerating pace, with 10 million square metres already installed in China and yearly sales

Figure 2.2   Thermosyphon flat plate collector with direct connection to horizontal tank (courtesy of *Renewable Energy World*, March–April 2002)

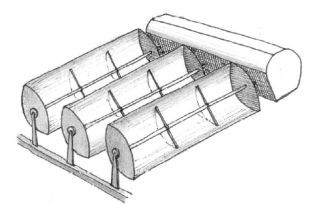

Figure 2.3   Parabolic trough collectors (SunTrack) with heat pipe absorber inserted directly into horizontal storage tank

of 3 million square metres. The market in China is five times larger than that in Europe. In 2001 China produced 20 million all-glass evacuated tube collectors. By 2003 the installed total was 50 million square metres. In its tenth five-year plan the government set a target of 100 million square metres by 2010.

Economics
Whilst this technology is one of the cheapest renewable options it is still not cost-effective weighed against fossil-based energy with a payback time of around 20 years. The market will only grow significantly at this stage if:

- there is direct or indirect government support for the technology
- following this intervention, the market expands to achieve economies of scale
- the product is of the highest quality and fitting procedures are simplified and standardized
- there is an adequate network of trained and accredited specialist installers
- complete roof modules incorporating solar collectors are made available to the construction industry for new build, making the marginal cost of the collectors relatively moderate.

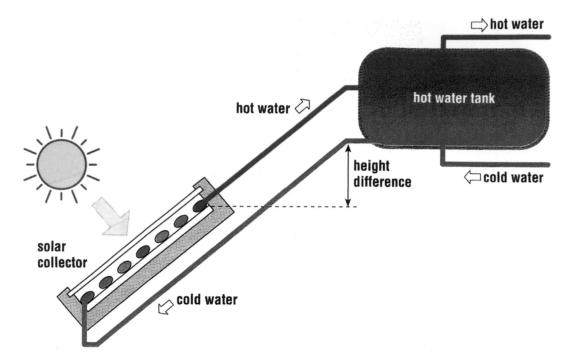

Figure 2.4   Solar thermosyphon system (courtesy of *Renewable Energy World*, March–April 2004)

Figure 2.5   Thermosyphon evacuated tube collectors with connection to header storage tank (courtesy of *Renewable Energy World*)

Solar buildings

Solar collectors are one of several renewable technologies that together make a solar building. It is essential that, from the earliest design stage, there is a symbiotic relationship between active solar and PVs, heat pumps and possibly small-scale wind turbines. 'Integrated design' is one of the slogans of the new millennium.

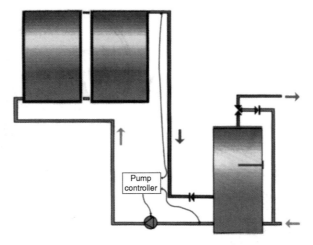

Figure 2.6   Open loop pumped circulation system (courtesy of *Renewable Energy World*)

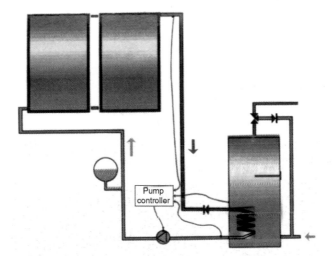

Figure 2.7   Closed loop (indirect) pumped circulation system with internal coil heat exchanger (courtesy of *Renewable Energy World*)

Well-designed solar houses can reduce energy demand by a factor of four against conventional homes. This has been demonstrated by the IEA Solar Heating Advanced Low Energy Buildings. With the addition of PV, it is possible for buildings to become net energy producers.

The effectiveness of the solar thermal applied to the existing housing stock is slightly reduced. Nevertheless, many buildings produced in northern Europe in the 1950s and 1960s are seriously in need of renovation. If solar technology is absorbed into the total overall cost and economies of scale are realized, the payback time should be considerably less than the normal twenty-year timescale.

In the UK there is an acute problem of poor-quality housing, much of it dating from the nineteenth century, which is associated with fuel poverty, ill health and substantial unnecessary winter deaths.

In the case of commercial buildings, cooling and lighting often outweigh heating as the dominant energy sink. This aspect of energy efficiency has been considered in some detail elsewhere.[2]

In Europe there are wide variations in the application of active solar heating. For example, Austria has almost $18\,m^2$ per 1000 inhabitants of installed capacity which is several orders of magnitude more than the UK, which has a climate that is not all that different from Austria.

Solar–gas combination boilers

The principle here is that a 240-litre tank is heated by flat plate solar collectors supplemented by a gas burner within the body of the cylinder. A heat exchanger coil in the upper half of the tank heats the central heating circuit. A production solar–gas combination boiler with $2.83\,m^2$ of solar collectors produces 4 GJ/year;[3] a $5.4\,m^2$ collector supplies 5.64 GJ/year. A test involving 25 units showed boiler efficiency of 90.1%. On average, consumers saved $650\,m^3$ of natural gas compared with conventional systems. At 2000 prices this gave a payback time of 13 years; at today's prices it will be much shorter. Another factor to consider is that it would be carbon neutral if biogas were employed (see Fig. 2.8).

Active district solar heating

Flat plate or evacuated tube solar heating collectors are a well-established technology for individual buildings, especially at the domestic scale. The next development is likely to

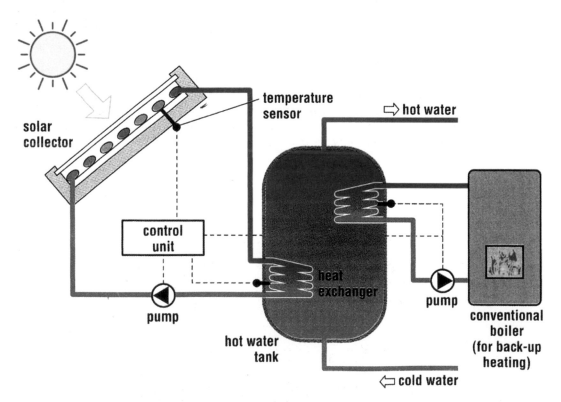

Figure 2.8 Mechanical circulation solar thermal system with back-up boiler (courtesy of Renewable Energy World, March–April 2004)

be the scaling up of this technology to help meet heating requirements at district level. According to Dirk Mangold of the University of Stuttgart, 'Central solar heating plants offer one of the most economic ways of providing thermal solar energy to housing estates for domestic hot water and room heating. Over 50% of the fossil-fuel demand of an ordinary district heating plant can be replaced by solar energy when seasonal heat storage is included in the plant.'[4]

District solar heating plants consist of a network of solar collectors which may be sited on ground level rigs next to a central heating substation. In urban situations it is more likely that solar collectors will be mounted on roofs. In Germany and Sweden there are available complete solar roof modules for construction purposes, complete with rafters and insulation. The flat plate collectors replace the tiles. Compared with a conventional roof the additional cost is €150–250/m² (excluding VAT) of flat plate area including all pipework and installation cost.

There are two basic systems of district solar heating: seasonal storage and diurnal storage.

Central solar heating plants for seasonal storage (CHSPSS)

Banking heat in summer to meet winter expenditure is the principle behind seasonal storage. There are four principal storage technologies.

1. *Aquifer heat storage:* Naturally occurring aquifers are charged with heat via wells during the warming season. In winter the system goes into reverse and the warmth distributed through the district network (see Fig. 2.9).
2. *Gravel/water heat storage:* A pit with a watertight plastic liner is filled with a gravel/water mix as the storage medium. The storage container is insulated at the sides and top, and base for small installations. Heat is fed into and drawn out of the storage tank both directly and indirectly (see Fig. 2.10(a)).
3. *Hot-water storage:* This comprises a steel or concrete insulated tank built partly or wholly into the ground (see Fig. 2.10(b))
4. *Duct heat storage:* Heat is stored in water-saturated soil. U-pipes are placed in vertical boreholes which are insulated near the surface. Heat is fed into and out of the ground via the U-pipes. Storage temperature can reach 85°C (Fig 2.10(c)).

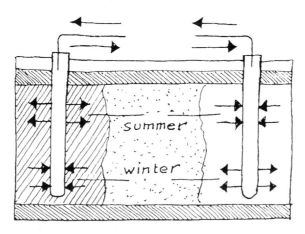

Figure 2.9   Aquifer heat storage

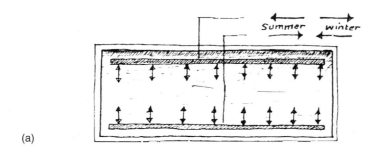

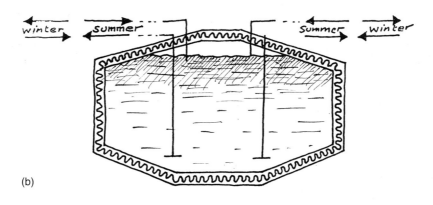

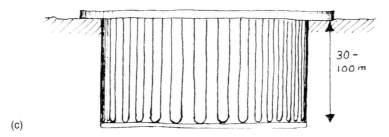

Figure 2.10   (a) Gravel/water heat storage; (b) hot water storage; (c) duct heat storage

Central solar plants for seasonal storage aim at a solar fraction of at least 50% of the total heat demand for space heating and domestic hot water for a housing estate of at least 100 apartments. The solar fraction is that part of the total annual energy demand which is met by solar energy.

In all these installations it is necessary to receive authorization from the relevant water authority.

By 2003 Europe had 45 MW of installed thermal power from solar collector areas of over 500 m². The ten largest installations in Europe are in Denmark, Sweden, Germany and the Netherlands, mostly serving housing complexes. Germany's first solar-assisted district

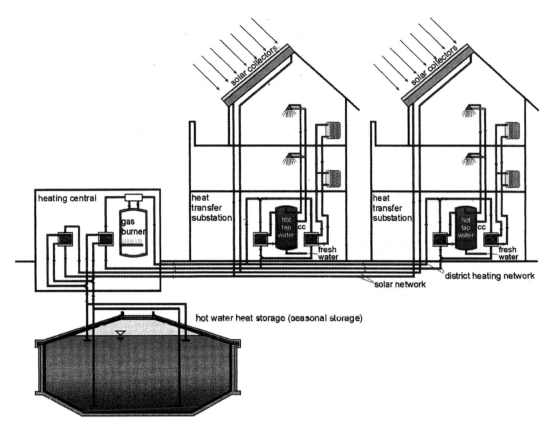

Figure 2.11   Diagram of CSHPSS system, Friedrichshafen (courtesy of *Renewable Energy World*)

heating projects, launched as part of a government research project 'Solarthermie 2000', were at Ravensburg and Neckarsulm. These have already proved valuable test beds for subsequent schemes.

One of the largest projects is at Friedrichshafen, and can serve to illustrate the system (see Fig. 2.11). The heat from $5600\,m^2$ of solar collectors on the roofs of eight housing blocks containing 570 apartments is transported to a central heating unit or substation. It is then distributed to the apartments as required. The heated living area amounts to $39,500\,m^2$.

Surplus summer heat is directed to the seasonal heat store which, in this case, is of the hot water variety, capable of storing $12,000\,m^3$. The scale of this storage facility is indicated by Fig. 2.12.

The heat delivery of the system amounts to 1915 MWh/year and the solar fraction is 47%. The month-by-month ratio between solar- and fossil-based energy indicates that from April to November inclusive, solar energy accounts for almost total demand being principally domestic hot water (see Fig. 2.13).

The Neckarsulm project is smaller, serving six multi-family homes, a school and a commercial centre, amounting to a heating area of $20,000\,m^2$. The roof-mounted solar collector area comes to $27,000\,m^2$ to satisfy a heat demand of 1663 MWh/year. In this instance the

Figure 2.12   Seasonal storage tank under construction, Friedrichshafen (courtesy of *Renewable Energy World*)

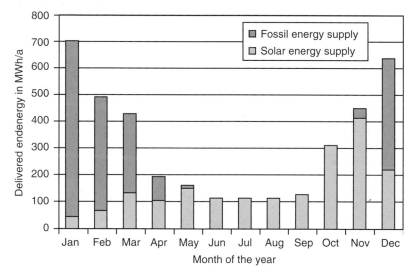

Figure 2.13   Monthly ratio of solar- to fossil-based energy at Friedrichshafen (courtesy of *Renewable Energy World*)

solar fraction is 50%. The storage facility is a duct heat storage tank with a capacity of $20,000\,m^3$ (see Fig. 2.14).

Central solar heating plant diurnal storage (CSHP)

In this case, the storage capacity is obviously much less, merely coping with a 24-hour demand. The demonstration project at Ravensburg supplies 29 terraced houses with hot

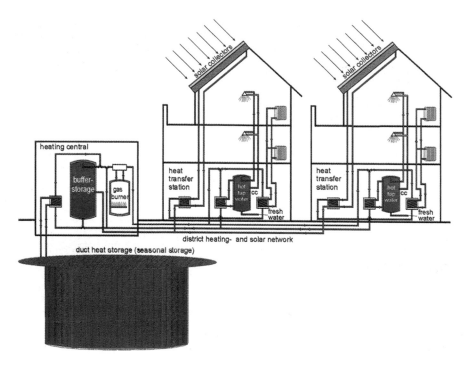

Figure 2.14 Diagram of the Neckarsulm project (courtesy of *Renewable Energy World*)

water and space heating via a four-pipe district heating network. It is calculated that this should meet 11% of the total heat requirement of the estate (see Fig. 2.15).

Solar systems with diurnal storage are mainly used to supply domestic hot water to large housing estates, large apartment blocks or hostels. They are designed to achieve a solar fraction of 80–100% in summer, representing 40–50% of annual heating demand in central and northern Europe.

Both seasonal and diurnal systems should be designed as part of a comprehensive energy efficiency programme involving insulation and rational energy conversion and supply. This can result in energy savings of 60% against the current norm.[5]

Solar thermal electricity

Solar energy is more evenly distributed across the sun belt of the planet than either wind or biomass. The downside is that deserts do not attract centres of population. However, as the world gradually switches to becoming a hydrogen-based energy economy, solar thermal electricity could be the key to substantial hydrogen production by electrolysis. African countries bordering the Mediterranean could greatly boost their economies by exporting solar hydrogen to Europe by tanker or pipeline. This may also be the future for the Gulf States (see Chapter 12).

In response to a challenge by the European Union in 1999 the Soltherm Europe Initiative was launched. Its aim was to install 15 million square metres of thermal solar collectors in Europe by 2004. The European Commission's White Paper, 'Energy for the Future', set a target of 100 million square metres across Europe by 2010.

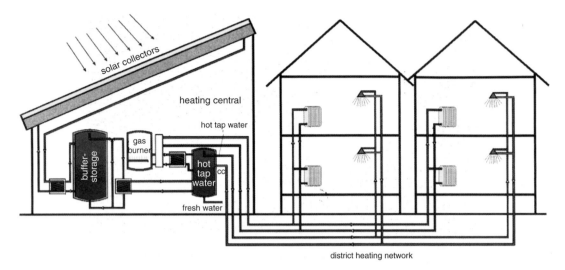

Figure 2.15   Diagram of the Ravensburg central solar heating plant diurnal storage project (courtesy of *Renewable Energy World*)

There are four key elements to solar thermal power technologies:

- *concentrator* – which captures and focuses solar radiation
- *receiver* – this absorbs the concentrated sunlight transferring the heat energy to a working fluid
- *transporter-storage* – which passes the fluid from the receiver to the power conversion system; in some systems a proportion of the thermal energy is stored for later use such as night-time
- *power conversion* – this is the generation phase via a heat engine such as a Stirling engine or steam engine.

There are two basic types of concentrator.

- *Parabolic trough collector*: This system comprises long parallel rows of concentrator modules using trough-shaped mirrors. It tracks the sun from east to west by rotating on a linear axis. The trough collector focuses sunlight onto an absorber pipe located along the focal line of the trough. A heat transfer fluid, typically oil-heated to 400°C or water to 520°C, is transported through the pipes to drive a conventional steam power generator (see Fig. 2.16).
- *Solar central receiver or 'power tower'*: In this instance an array of mirrors or 'heliostats' is arranged around a central axis, focusing solar radiation onto the focal point of the array. A receiver situated on a tower at the focal point transfers the solar heat to a power block in the form of a steam generator (see Fig. 2.17).

Research is being conducted into ultra-high-energy towers which can heat pressurized air to over 1000°C then to be fed into the gas turbines of combined cycle systems.

A version produced in the US by STM Power of Michigan links their 'SunDish' tower system to a Stirling engine to produce electricity.

The solar collector or 'SunDish' consists of an array of mirrors which tracks the path of the sun, focusing its rays on a thermal concentrator. The solar energy is focused onto a hemispherical absorber in the engine's heat pipe receiver. The heat pipe receiver transfers heat at between 300 and 800°C to the Stirling engine, which is hermetically sealed, producing daytime electricity with zero emissions. At night the engine is heated by a range of possible fuels

Figure 2.16   Solar thermal parabolic trough collector (courtesy of Caddet)

Figure 2.17   Solar thermal generator (courtesy of Caddet)

including landfill gas, wood chippings and biogas from an anaerobic digester. An operating cost of about 3.2 cents per kWh is claimed.

Where there is a high level and rate of solar radiation, multiple dish mirrors focusing on a Stirling engine have been producing grid-quality electricity for over 25,000 hours in the west of the USA (see Fig. 2.18).

A criticism of solar thermal plants is that they are only effective in the day-time. The Australian National University has met this challenge head-on by developing a sun dish

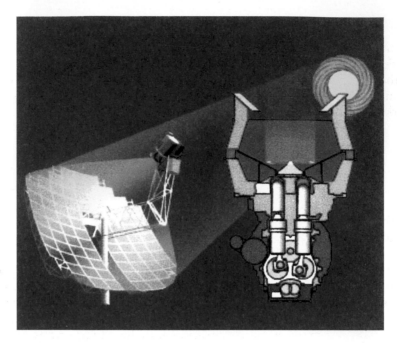

Figure 2.18   Solar Energy Systems Solar Dish Stirling technology (courtesy of Solar Energy Systems Inc.)

which focuses radiation onto a thermochemical reactor containing ammonia. Under the intense heat the ammonia is broken down into hydrogen and nitrogen which is then stored at ambient temperature. It is stored in lengths of former natural gas pipelines. When needed the gases are recombined using an adapted industrial ammonia synthesis reactor. The 500°C of heat generated by the recombination is used to generate steam for a conventional power plant. The beauty of the system is that the gases are constantly recirculated within a closed loop. The leaders of the research team, Dr Keith Lovegrove and Dr Andreas Luzzi, claim that a solar field the size of a suburb would power a city the size of Canberra.

A major advantage of solar thermal systems is that they can be integrated into existing conventional power technologies. This will ease the transition to a fully renewable electricity supply system in the long-term future. In large measure this will be achieved by the re-powering of existing fossil fuel plants.

There is confidence in the industry that future developments of this technology will deliver much higher efficiencies whilst driving down costs of electricity to a level that will compare favourably with conventional power plants.

Solar thermal – the future

Solar thermal is still suffering from the problem that it has emerged out of the plumbing sector of industry, resulting in certain mindsets which inhibit innovation. The following are some pointers to the way ahead.

Modular design

Solar heaters must become an off-the-shelf item, with standardized connectors and in modules based on the amount of hot water required by one person.

Simplified design

The installation procedures should be foolproof, making wrong connections inherently impossible. For example, many manufacturers still do not offer a standardized sleeve at the top end of the absorber to enable a sensor to be correctly inserted. Design rationalization would not only speed up installation time and reduce costs but also bring solar panels into the DIY market.

Legionella

This is a waterborne bacterium that multiplies at between 40 and 50°C which is the average temperature of water storage including solar. It is potentially fatal if inhaled, for instance when showering. In some countries regulations require a minimum storage temperature of 70°C to be achieved at least once a day. This is the blanket-bombing technique which has a negative impact on the efficiency of the collectors due to scaling problems which arise at over 60°C.

There are other possibly more effective ways of killing the bacteria. Ultraviolet light at high intensity destroys the bacteria's ability to reproduce and is frequently used for water purification. It is still not used in solar thermal systems. Used in combination with ultrasonic waves or anodic oxidation it should remove the source of the problem like biofilms in the pipes. This would be more efficient than achieving a high temperature for part of a day.

Antifreeze

It is standard practice to include an antifreeze agent in the collector for obvious reasons. The antifreeze agents are toxic, expensive, have a poor ability to carry heat and can change viscosity which can cause leaks. To avoid the need for antifreeze, some systems automatically drain off when there is not enough solar gain. Another approach would be to design an absorber which can accommodate the expansion accompanying freezing. It could be that the time taken to melt the ice as the sun rises would be compensated for by the higher efficiency of a system without antifreeze.

Storage

It was stated earlier that storage tanks should be insulated. There is still insufficient importance attached to this aspect of the system. Just as vacuum tube collectors are now available, so the next logical step is to have vacuum storage tanks which would maximize heat retention.

Solar control units

There is still some way to go to make these user-friendly. They tend to be difficult to handle and are expensive for the function they perform, which is often merely to control a pump's on–off position. Often faults in a system are not discovered until an excessive heating bill arrives from the utility. Pressure, temperature and flow rates could easily be displayed in a living room with a red light indicating a fault.

Intelligent systems

We are in the age when computers can learn by feedback. Intelligent systems could learn about consumers' behaviour and adjust heat output accordingly. For example, it would be possible to adjust the collector pump to reduce its rate of flow in order to increase the water temperature to coincide with the regular time occupants take a shower. It may only require 20 litres of enhanced temperature to meet this need. Over time an intelligent system will learn to finely tune supply to demand, thereby minimizing the involvement of a back-up heater.

Improvements are often avoided by being hit with the argument of cost-effectiveness. This is often an excuse for avoiding changing designs and manufacturing techniques. In the case of solar thermal, simplified and standardized installation procedures should consider-ably reduce the 21% of total system cost currently spent on installation. Add to this the fact that the system is more efficient and faults detected instantly, then the added costs should easily be offset, bringing them overall close to the heat production costs of conventional energy sources.

A major cost burden is imposed by the use of copper for piping. The high cost of copper is unlikely to change. In fact it is a commodity likely to rise as demand increases, ironically driven partly by the growing popularity of renewables. Plastic pipes are becoming more common. New materials such as reinforced silicon hose, which is gas-tight and which can cope with high temperatures and offers a degree of expansion, will be a suitable alternative. It is flexible, which means that installation procedures are simplified. Add some clever con-nectors which can be installed on site and materials like silicon will capture the market.

Finally, the manufacture of solar thermal devices needs to make the transition from small-scale labour-intensive small and medium enterprises (SME) operations to high-out-put industrial mass production using specialized component manufacturers. This will not only change the image of the technology but would also cope with its predicted rapid growth as the energy infrastructure becomes increasingly stressed due to geopolitical fac-tors and problems of security of supply.

For the information on the future I am indebted to Cornelius Suchy, renewable energy specialist with MVV consultants and Engineers, GmbH.

Notes

1. peta joules $= 10^{15}$ joules; one watt $=$ one joule per second; one joule $= 6.242 \times 10^{18}$ electron-volts
2. Smith, P. F. (2001) *Architecture in a Climate of Change,* Architectural Press, Oxford
3. gigajoule $=$ joules 10^9 (billion)
4. *Renewable Energy World,* May–June 2001
5. The data in this section were drawn from a paper by Dirk Mangold in *Renewable Energy World,* May–June 2001

3 Low energy techniques for cooling

The cooling of buildings is one of the largest of all energy sinks and therefore a major contributor to CO_2 emissions. This chapter considers a range of alternatives which fall into two categories:

- technologies which involve an external or stand-alone source of energy
- systems which are integrated into the structure and fabric of a building

Ground coupling using air

In the UK the ground temperature below 2 metres is fairly constant, ranging between 10 and 14°C. Ideally the soil temperature should be 12°C or less. This makes it a suitable source of cooling in summer and possibly warmth in winter. The system operates by passing air through a network of pipes set at 2–5 m below ground. The soil temperature is roughly the same as the average yearly ambient temperature.

Best results are obtained when the circuit of pipes is positioned within gravel or sand and below the water table.

A number of factors influence the design of such a system:

- actual soil temperature
- velocity of the air through the pipes
- diameter of the pipes
- extent of the underground network
- conductivity of the soil
- moisture level of the soil.

The cooled air can be used directly as a cooling agent or it can provide pre-cooled air for conventional ventilation or air conditioning.

In the context of this technology it is necessary to check for ground pollution, especially radon gas (see Fig. 3.1).

Groundwater/aquifer cooling and warming

Alternatives to full air conditioning with chillers that make heavy demands on electricity and fossil fuel for space heating are coming increasingly into prominence. One option is

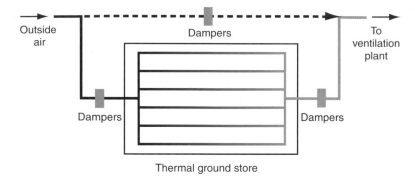

Figure 3.1   Ground source air cooling (courtesy of Building Research Establishment (BRE))

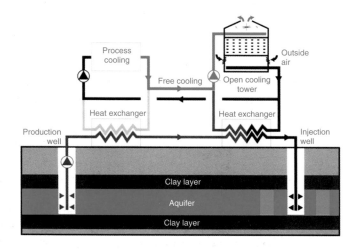

Figure 3.2   Aquifer cold water/warm water storage system (courtesy of Caddet)

aquifer thermal energy storage (ATES). This uses water from an underground well to cool either a building or an industrial process. Once the water has taken up the heat from the building etc., it can be returned to a second warm well and used to pre-heat ventilation air in winter.

Two boreholes are drilled to a depth of between 30 and 150 metres. The wells should be between 100 and 150 m apart.

Where there is no movement of groundwater ATES uses layers of water for cold and heat storage. In summer cool groundwater passes through a heat exchanger where it cools the water system of the building which, in turn, cools incoming air in an air-handling unit.

The groundwater, having absorbed the building's heat, is injected into the warm well. During the winter the system is put into reverse.

It is estimated that ATES can achieve 60–80% energy savings compared with conventional air conditioning. It has quite a short payback time to recover the extra investment of 2–8 years (see Fig. 3.2).

In situations where there is groundwater movement the system can be used as a heat source or sink for a heat pump (see below).

In the UK the extraction and use of groundwater is subject to approval by the Environment Agency.

Evaporative cooling

Evaporative cooling exploits the principle that molecules of a substance in a vapour state contain much more energy than the same molecules in a liquid state. The amount of heat needed to change a substance like water into a vapour is its latent heat of evaporation. The heat is removed from the liquid and transferred to the vapour, causing cooling of surfaces in the process. This is the cooling system employed by nature in humans to lower the body temperature through perspiration.[1]

Direct evaporative cooling is achieved when incoming air is blown directly across a wetted medium or through a water spray. In this instance evaporative cooling provides 'sensible' cooling, i.e. experienced by the senses, whilst increasing the latent heat content of the air. The process is called 'adiabatic cooling' where the sensible heat removed from the air equals the latent heat absorbed by the water evaporated as the heat of vaporization.

This method of cooling can be created by intelligent landscaping, as when incoming air first passes over the surface of an external mass of water. An example where this technique is to be seen is at the University of Nottingham. In its Jubilee Campus the prevailing winds cross an artificial lake before being directed into the building by an inclined plane of glazing.[2]

Indirect evaporative cooling occurs when exhaust air is cooled using evaporative techniques and then used to cool the incoming air by being passed through a heat exchanger.

The Malta Stock Exchange offers an interesting variation on the theme of evaporative cooling. The interest lies in the fact that it is an existing chapel converted to this new function. Being a historic building, its walls have high thermal mass. The architect chosen was Brian Ford of WSP Environmental and formerly of Short Ford and Partners, who designed the celebrated Queen's Engineering Building at Leicester de Montfort University. He opted for a passive downdraught evaporative cooling (PDEC) solution. The major advantage of PDEC is that it is driven by buoyancy dynamics alone, removing the need for mechanical assistance.

A raised roof ridge accommodates the misting jets and cooling pipes. Fresh air is drawn through centre pivot vents in the side of the ridge which is then cooled by evaporation. This sets up a downdraught, cooling the atrium below. In summer, automatic high-level vents allow the night-time air entering at low level to pre-cool the building.

In the event that internal relative humidity level is above 65% the evaporation nozzles are automatically switched off and chilled water is directed to the cooling pipes. This causes cool air to descend into the atrium whilst the warm air rises up the sides of the atrium to be cooled and then descend. Energy has to be used to chill the water but there are no fans which typically use 30% of the energy of an air conditioning system. There is also no ductwork or air handling units.

Thermal modelling predictions indicated that electricity savings of 50% would be realized against a conventional air conditioning system (see Fig. 3.3).

Air handling systems which involve the warming of water carry a theoretical risk of legionella. Evaporative cooling can create pre-cooling of ambient air for dry air coolers. This lowers the temperature of the water in the system which reduces the risk of this disease compared to a wet cooling tower.

Advantages of evaporative cooling include:

- the fact that it can be combined with conventional systems
- the heat exchanger in indirect systems can be used for heat recovery in winter
- if the exchanger is located within the exhaust air pathway.

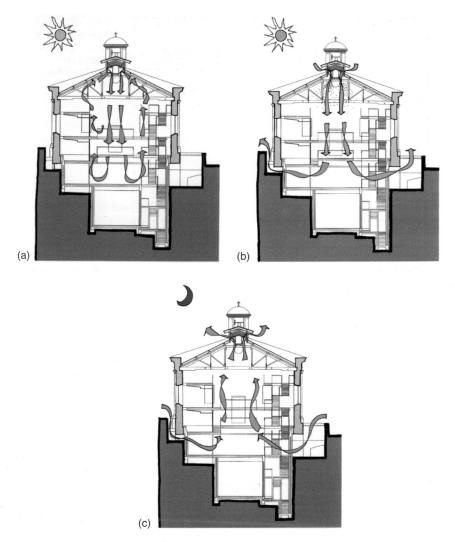

Figure 3.3   Sections and ventilation paths, Malta Stock Exchange. (a) summer cooling to the atrium is provided by a combination of passive evaporation, cooling coils and night-time cooling. When outside temperature is high and relative humidity below 60%, misting nozzles operate and cooling air is drawn through side vents in the ridge. (b) above relative humidity of 65%, nozzles switch off and chilled water in the cooling pipes takes over the cooling function. (c) at night, ridge vents opened and cool air is drawn from low level, rising by stack effect to exit at high level, pre-cooling the structure in the process (courtesy of WSP Environmental)

Phase change cooling

A phase change material (PCM) is one which changes its state from solid to liquid when subjected to heating and vice versa when cooled. Water is the obvious example. When it changes from a solid (ice) to a liquid it absorbs large amounts of heat before it shows any increase in temperature. A PCM which changes its state at temperatures around the range for thermal comfort is ideal for moderating temperature in buildings. One such material is sodium sulphate and its variant, Glauber's salt, which is a decahydrate of sodium sulphate. Glauber was

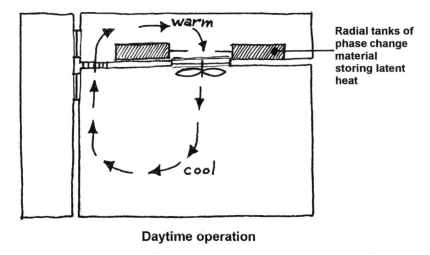

Daytime operation

Figure 3.4   Phase change cooling. Fan draws warm air from the room which passes over phase change tanks cooling in the process as PCM changes from solid to liquid

a German Chemist born in 1604, yet another case of an early discovery waiting centuries to find its true 'vocation'. It changes from a solid to a liquid at around 28°C, absorbing large amounts of heat and thus cooling the air in its vicinity. The reverse operation creates heat when the PCM returns to the solid.

A variation on the theme of phase change cooling has been produced by researchers at Nottingham University Institute of Building Technology. The underlying principle still uses a chemical heat sink to soak up the heat in the air and pump cool air into a building. It is a highly energy-efficient system, using only a fraction of the energy consumed by conventional air conditioning. It is a system particularly suited to temperate climes where a few degrees of cooling can achieve comfort temperature.

The system invented by David Etheridge and David Rae draws daytime warm external air by fan over an array of fluid filled heat pipes. The pipes conduct heat to storage modules containing a solid PCM. The PCMs located in the ceiling void absorb the heat as they slowly melt during the day, providing cool ventilation air (see Fig. 3.4).

During the night the opposite occurs. Shutters to the outside air are opened and the fan reverses direction to draw the cool air over the PCMs, causing the material to solidify. The heat generated in the process is dumped outside the building (see Fig. 3.5).

The whole operation works on the principle that latent heat is stored in the PCMs. Their temperature hardly changes throughout the cycle since it is their latent heat capacity which brings about the change in air temperature.

The system is capable of being fine-tuned to suit specific circumstances by adding chemicals which change the melting point of the PCM.

The researchers claim that this method of cooling is more agreeable to the occupants than conventional air conditioning, which often produces zones of excessive cooling whilst, at the same time, excluding the possibility of receiving natural ventilation via open windows. The Nottingham system is not affected by being supplemented by extra natural ventilation.

Perhaps the greatest virtue of the system in the context of the Kyoto Protocol is that its energy costs are merely one sixteenth those of conventional air conditioning with obvious CO_2 emission benefits.

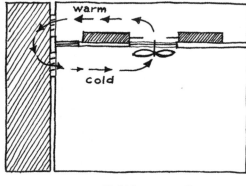

Nighttime operation

Figure 3.5   Phase change cooling. At night the fan reverses direction and the external vents open. Cool air is drawn over the PCM which cools and solidifies

Daytime operation

Another system for solar cooling is being developed in the Nottingham laboratories. Evacuated tube solar collectors heat water to around 110°C. The resultant high-pressure steam is expelled at around mach 2. The steam passes through an ejector where the Venturi effect causes the pressure to drop. A liquid refrigerant is fed to the ejector where it vaporizes under the vacuum created in the ejector, causing a cooling effect which is transmitted to the internal space. This adiabatic cooling drops the temperature to −1°C. The low-pressure steam exiting the ejector is condensed and the water recirculated. In the Nottingham project the evacuated heat pipe array collects 13 kW of solar heat and converts it to 6 kW of refrigeration. The system is backed up by natural gas when the temperature is high but cloudy conditions cut out the solar gain. This system is patented but not yet licensed.

Desiccant dehumidification and evaporative cooling

In some environments a combination of high temperature and high humidity defies a remedy by conventional air conditioning which is biased towards temperature rather than humidity. Dehumidification is merely a by-product of bringing the temperature down to below the dew point of the air, causing condensation.

A desiccant is a hygroscopic material, liquid or solid, which can extract moisture from humid air, gas or liquids. Liquid desiccants work by absorption where moisture is taken up by chemical action. Solid desiccants have a large internal area capable of absorbing significant quantities of water by capillary action. Examples of efficient desiccants are

- silica gel
- activated alumina
- lithium salts
- triethylene glycol.

This method of dehumidification requires a heating stage in the process. This is to dry or regenerate the desiccant material and requires a temperature range of 60–90°C. One option is to supply the heat by means of evacuated tube solar collectors, backed up by natural gas

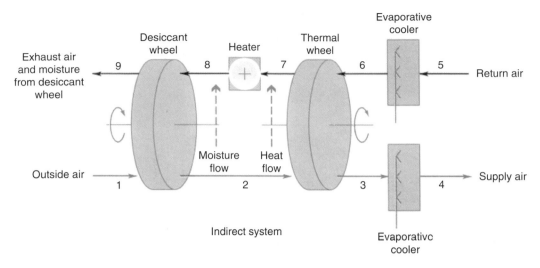

Figure 3.6 Desiccant wheel and thermal wheel dehumidifying and cooling

when insolation is inadequate. Alternatively waste heat, for example from a Stirling CHP unit, may be exploited.

As a full alternative to air conditioning, desiccant dehumidification can be used in conjunction with evaporative cooling. After being dried by the revolving desiccant wheel the air passes through a heat exchanger such as a thermal wheel for cooling. If necessary further cooling may be achieved by an evaporative cooler before the air is supplied to the building.

The exhaust air at room temperature also passes through an evaporative cooler and then through the thermal wheel, chilling it in the process. This enables the thermal wheel to cool the supply air. After passing through the thermal wheel the air is heated and directed through the desiccant wheel to remove moisture and then expelled to the atmosphere.

There are problems with the system. It is not amenable to precise temperature and humidity control and it is not so efficient in dry climates. On the positive side it is providing a full fresh air system (see Fig. 3.6).

Solar-assisted desiccant dehumidification with air conditioning

In certain extreme environments it is necessary to couple desiccant dehumidification with conventional air conditioning. However, the pre-conditioning of the air reduces the load on the air conditioning plant.

As in the case above the system has two air pathways, incoming and outgoing. The incoming path draws external air through a slowly revolving desiccant wheel which draws off the moisture and delivers the dried air to the air conditioner. In the other path, hot air from the building is further heated by evacuated-tube solar collectors serving a heat exchanger to regenerate the desiccant material in the revolving wheel before being ejected from the building.

This system is especially appropriate for restaurants/kitchens which can experience extremes of both temperature and humidity[3] (see Fig. 3.7).

A further advantage of this system is that it can remove pollutants from the air. It also has the benefit of being able to offer a continual supply of fresh air, unlike full air conditioning.

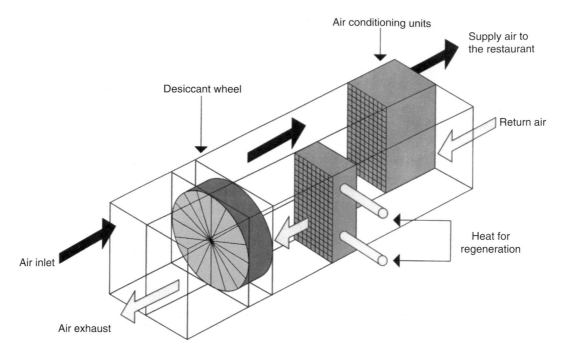

Figure 3.7   Desiccant wheel dehumidifying and cooling system courtesy of (*Caddet Renewable Energy Newsletter*, March 2000)

Refrigeration

The inventor of refrigeration technology was Albert Einstein, better known for solving the problems of the universe. This innovation was responsible for the explosion in the sale of domestic refrigerators which occurred in the 1930s. The compressor refrigerator is based on a thermodynamic cycle whereby a gas is compressed mechanically, causing it to heat up. After discharging its heat the gas, still under pressure, liquefies. The liquid is allowed to expand by lowering the pressure. In the process it evaporates, absorbing heat from its surroundings. The relationship between the cooling capacity and the power needed to achieve it is called the coefficient of performance (CoP). For well-designed machines this can approach 100%. In a solar linked system, PVs could provide electricity for the compressor.

Ammonia-absorption cooling

In the case of ammonia absorption cooling (Fig. 3.8) the operation relies on the fact that ammonia is soluble in cold water but not in hot water. When a solution of water and ammonia is heated, ammonia vapour is driven off at high pressure.

If this gas is then cooled in a condenser to ambient temperature it becomes a liquid. This pure liquid ammonia is brought into contact with a small amount of hydrogen gas in an evaporator. This causes the ammonia to revert again to a gas, absorbing heat from its surroundings in the process. This is the cooling phase of the process.

The ammonia–hydrogen mix is then brought into contact with water at the absorber at ambient temperature. At this temperature the ammonia is able to dissolve into the water, leaving the pure hydrogen to be returned to the evaporator for the process to begin again.

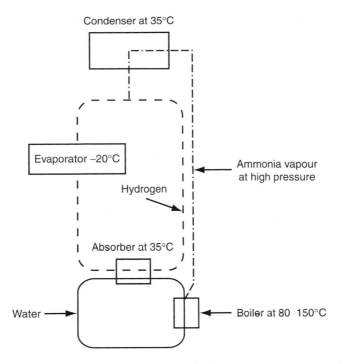

Figure 3.8   Ammonia absorption cooling system

There is no mechanical support for the circulation process which is driven by a 'bubble pump'. This comprises a narrow vertical heated vessel where bubbles form, lifting the liquid in the process. The most common application of bubble pump technology is the espresso coffee machine. This pump is cheap and maintenance-free.

The technology has some inherent problems such as the fact that if the boiler does not reach a critical temperature it does not drive off all the ammonia as a vapour which, in turn, undermines the effectiveness of the purification of the hydrogen. As the evaporation temperature of the ammonia in the evaporator depends on the vapour pressure of the ammonia in the hydrogen, an inadequate boiler temperature would significantly reduce the cooling efficiency of the system.

The basic system requires the boiler which heats the ammonia–water mix to reach a temperature of 150°C. In solar energy terms this can only be achieved by solar concentrators. Researchers in the Technical University of Vienna redesigned the cycle, inserting an extra loop called a 'bypass' which makes it possible to extract much more ammonia from the ammonia–water solution at a relatively lower temperature than was previously possible. As a result, a boiler temperature of 75–80°C brings about the necessary evaporation of ammonia. This brings the technology within the range of normal evacuated tube solar collectors for providing the heat. This is the ideal heat source since it is at its most abundant during the summer when cooling is in greatest demand.

To provide space cooling a fan drives ambient air over the evaporator to be ducted from there throughout the building.

The heat source could also be spare heat from a CHP system driven by an internal combustion engine, a microturbine or a Stirling engine (see Fig. 3.8).

Thermionic cooling

It was in 1883 that Thomas Edison discovered this phenomenon but it was not until 1994 that Gerald Mahan published a rather pessimistic paper on the prospects for this form of refrigeration. It is based on an electrical device called a vacuum diode which goes under the name of the Cool Chip. It contains two thin films separated by a narrow vacuum layer. If a voltage is put across the gap the most energetic electrons on the negative side 'boil off', carrying their kinetic energy to the positive side of the chip. As the hottest electrons migrate, the negative side or cathode cools, opening up the prospect of chemical-free refrigeration. The extra energy in the electrons reaching the positive anode is merely dissipated as heat. This is the basis of thermionics.

A British company called Borealis is optimistic that this technology has considerable potential, offering 80% efficiency as against the 30–50% of a compressor refrigerator. A panel of 25 chips covering $5\,cm^2$ would operate a typical domestic fridge using about 15 W of electricity. It has the advantage of being silent, with no moving parts and therefore virtually maintenance-free. It remains to be seen if the technology can be scaled up to provide cooling for buildings. Indirectly it has the potential for reducing the cooling load in buildings by cooling microprocessors and other electrical equipment that make a significant contribution to the heat build-up in offices.[4]

Night-time cooling

At the start of the chapter it was stated that there is a category of cooling which uses the building fabric as a component of the system. The most elementary is with natural ventilation.

With natural ventilation

This method makes use of the exposed thermal mass of a building to be cooled by the outside air during the night. Exposed concrete floors are the most effective cooling medium. Vaulted or coffered soffits offer the maximum radiant surface. The cooling stored in the fabric is released as radiant cooling or an air stream directed over surfaces during the day. Vents or windows are automatically opened at night to admit the cool air. During the day warm air is vented to the atmosphere. The fact that it is radiant cooling may allow the air temperature to be slightly higher than the norm whilst still maintaining comfort conditions.

Night cooling of a high thermal mass structure can offset about $20–30\,W/m^2$ of heat gain during the day, reducing the peak temperature by about 2–3°C.

The system is optimized if there is cross ventilation and internal solar gains are kept to a minimum. The method works best if there is a large diurnal temperature range with night temperature below 20°C. Also, the best results are achieved in narrow open plan spaces, say 15 m maximum between façades. There is the limitation that heat gains should not exceed $30\,W/m^2$.

With mechanical ventilation

In this case the cooling potential of night-time air is optimized by being forced through the building fabric by fans. At the same time it assists in expelling warm air during the day. The system has the advantage that it eliminates the need to have open windows either day or night. It also offers control over the supply and extract air flow.

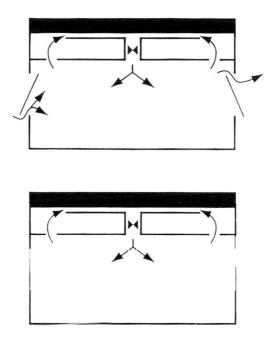

Figure 3.9   Enhanced surface heat transfer system (courtesy of BRE)

A variation is described as the 'enhanced surface heat transfer system'. A perforated metal sheet is applied to the underside of the floor slab leaving an air gap. Air is mechanically forced into the gap, creating turbulent air currents which appreciably improve the heat transfer between the air and the slab, maximizing night-time cooling. The external air can be ducted directly to the gap or emitted into the room and then recirculated through the ceiling gap. As with natural ventilation the night-time temperature should be below 20°C. However, the heat gains that can be accommodated can increase to $50\,\text{W/m}^2$ (see Fig. 3.9).

Hollow core slab

Precast concrete floors with integral connected ducts can effectively move either cool or warm air throughout a building. The air is in contact with the thermal capacity of the concrete before entering the occupied space. This is a highly efficient means of achieving a high rate of air to slab heat transfer and vice versa and therefore the charging and discharging of cooling. The soffit of the slab should be exposed to effect maximum heat exchange with the occupied area. In this condition the hollow core slab can offset heat gains by up to $50\,\text{W/m}^2$. One of the best-known proprietary systems using this technique is Termodeck from Sweden (see Fig. 3.10). There will be a further reference to this system in Chapter 15.

Chilled beams and ceiling

Water is the heat transfer medium in this technology, circulating at the relatively high temperature of 16°C. Chilled beams create convective air movement to cool a room. In chilled ceilings a flat soffit panel provides radiant and convective cooling.

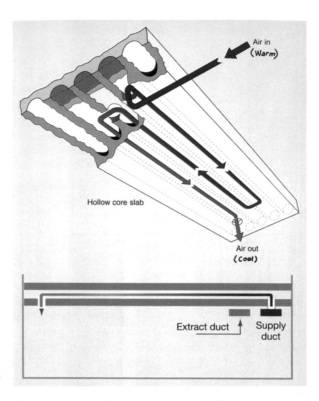

Figure 3.10   Hollow slab natural ventilation (courtesy of BRE)

Chilled beams can provide about 60 W/m² of cooling water at 16°C and a room temperature of 26°C.

Chilled ceilings provide roughly 40 W/m² assuming 50% active area, otherwise as for chilled beams.

Notes

1.   Randall Thomas, E. (ed) (1996) *Environmental Design*, Spon, pp. 12–13
2.   Smith, P. (2005) *Architecture in a Climate of Change*, 2nd edition, Architectural Press, Oxford, pp. 152–53
3.   *Caddet Renewable Energy Newsletter*, April 1995
4.   *New Scientist*, 'Boiling Fridges', 24 January 1998, pp. 30–31

4 Geothermal energy

Heat contained within the planet causes macrogeological events like earthquakes, volcanoes and tectonic movement. Geothermal energy in the context of this book refers to that small fraction of the Earth's heat which can be converted to useful energy. Most of this heat is generated by decaying radioactive isotopes within the Earth's mantle.

The rate of increase of temperature according to depth in the ground is called the 'geothermal gradient' and averages 2.5 to 3.0°C per 100 m of depth. Modern drilling techniques can penetrate up to 10 km.

Where there are active geothermal areas this gradient can increase by a factor of ten, producing temperatures above 300°C at 500 to 1000 m. This occurs where there is an upward intrusion of high-temperature rocks from the magma belt. In such circumstances a temperature of around 600°C can be expected at depths from 5 to 10 km. This would provide high-pressure steam. However, useful geothermal energy is available at the normal geothermal gradient.

This heat has to be brought to the surface. Geothermal springs do this spontaneously. More often, water has to be injected into the hot, permeable rocks known as the 'thermal reservoir', where it circulates, absorbing heat in the process. If there are several geothermal wells in a vicinity, this is described as a 'thermal field' (see Fig. 4.1).

An advantage of geothermal energy is that it is independent of climate or seasonal/diurnal variation. The capacity factor of geothermal plants is often in excess of 90%, producing energy at a price which is lower than most other renewable technologies.

Geothermal electricity

According to one authority, geothermal represents 42% of the electricity produced by the combination of wind, solar, tidal and geothermal. Electricity generation mainly involves conventional steam turbines which operate at a minimum of 150°C. There are two principal types of steam turbine, described below.

Atmospheric exhaust turbine

This is a relatively straightforward technology which is economical to install. Its output usually ranges between 2.5 and 5 MWe (electricity).

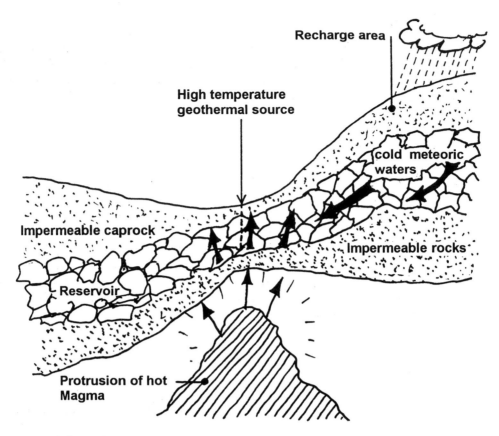

Figure 4.1   Schematic diagram of the geothermal system

Condensing turbines

This technology has more auxiliary equipment than atmospheric exhaust plants and is much larger with output reaching 100 MWe. It is more expensive pro rata due to its complexity, but, by way of compensation, it only uses half the quantity of steam per kWh compared with atmospheric exhaust plants.

Technical advances have made it possible to generate electricity with fluid temperatures as low as 80–90°C.

The International Geothermal Association (IGA) estimates that worldwide electricity-generating capacity from geothermal sources is over 8000 MWe, producing 50 TWh per year. This is expected to rise to 11,400 MWe by 2005. In addition to this there is the direct heat energy production. The estimated ultimate potential for high temperature geothermal electricity is 36,600 TWh per year. For heat alone, the global estimate is 14 million TJ (IGA).

Direct heat applications

As mentioned, medium to low temperature geothermal resources occur almost anywhere in the world and these have a use as sources of direct heat. Fifty-eight countries use geothermal energy in this way, amounting to an installed capacity of 15,145 MWt (thermal).

Heat pumps

One of the most significant areas of application is in combination with heat pumps. There has been a rapid improvement in heat pump technology, especially in the USA. Over the last five years the number of geothermal ground-source heat pumps has grown by 59% with most of the expansion in the USA and Europe. In 2001 there were over half a million ground-source heat pump installations in 26 countries.[1]

Environmental impact

Despite claims to the contrary, it is virtually impossible to produce and transform energy without some carbon dioxide emissions. A survey of over 5000 MW installed capacity of geothermal emitted an average of 65 g CO_2 per kWh. This compares with 450 g/kWh for gas, 906 g/kWh for oil and 1042 g/kWh for coal, excluding the embodied energy in plant and equipment as well as carbon miles for the transportation of oil and coal. So, geothermal advocates are justified in their claim that it is one of the cleanest sources of energy.

At a guess, geothermal-boosted ground-source heat pumps will lead the field in low-energy technology for buildings. It is relatively low cost, economical to run, insulated from the vagaries of weather and climate and changes in temperature and reliably produces heat in winter and cooling in summer. If PVs with battery backup provide the power for pumps and compressors then it really is a zero-energy system in operation.

Heat pumps are an offshoot of refrigeration technology and are capable of providing both heat and cooling. They exploit the principle that certain chemicals absorb heat when they are condensed into a liquid and release heat when they evaporate into a gas.

There are several different refrigerants that can be used for space heating and cooling with widely varying global warming potential (GWP). Refrigerants which have an ozone-depleting potential are now banned. Currently, refrigerants which have virtually zero GWP on release include ammonia, which is one of the most prevalent.

The heating and cooling capacity of the refrigerant is enhanced by the extraction of warmth or 'coolth' from an external medium – earth, air or water.

The most efficient is the geothermal heat pump (GHP), which originated in the 1940s. This is another technology which goes back a long way but which is only now realizing its potential as a technology for the future.

It exploits the relative warmth of the earth for both heating and cooling. The principle of the GHP is that it does not create heat; it transports it from one area to another. The main benefit of this technology is that it uses up to 50% less electricity than conventional electrical heating or cooling. A GHP uses one unit of electricity to move between three and four units of heat from the earth.

Most ground-coupled heat pumps adopt the closed-loop system whereby a high-density polyethylene pipe filled with a water and antifreeze mix, which acts as a heat transporter, is buried in the ground. It is laid in a U configuration either vertically or horizontally. The vertical pipes descend to about a 100 m depth; the horizontal loop is laid at a minimum of 2 m depth.

The horizontal type is most common in residential situations where there is usually adequate open space and because it incurs a much lower excavation cost than the alternative. The only problem is that, even at a 2 m depth, the circuit can be affected by solar gain or rainfall evaporation. In each case the presence of moving ground water improves performance.

Ground Coupled Heat Pumps (GCHP) a.k.a. closed loop heat pumps

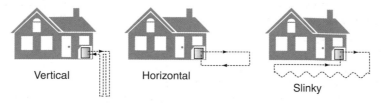

Groundwater Heat Pumps (GWHP) a.k.a. open loop heat pumps

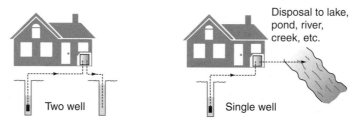

Surface water Heat Pumps (SWHP) a.k.a. lake or pond loop heat pumps

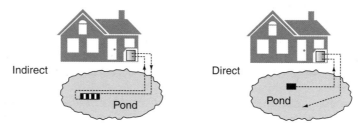

Figure 4.2   Heat pump variations (source: Kensa Engineering)

Usually the lowest cost option is to use water in a pond, lake or river as the heat transfer medium. The supply pipe is run underground from the building and coiled into circles at least 1.75 m below the surface (see Fig. 4.2).

Dr Robin Curtis (GeoScience Ltd) considers heat pumps to be analogous to rechargeable batteries that are permanently connected to a trickle charger. The battery is the ground-loop array which has to be large enough, together with a matched compressor, to meet the heating/cooling load of a building. The energy trickle comes from the surrounding land which recharges the volume of ground immediately surrounding the loop. If the energy removed from the ground exceeds the ground's regeneration capacity, the system ceases to function, so it is essential that demand is matched to the ground capacity.

At present, ground-coupled heat pumps have a coefficient of performance (COP) between 3 and 4, which means that for every kilowatt of electricity, they produce 3 to 4 kilowatts of useful heat. The theoretical ultimate COP for heat pumps is 14. In the future a COP of 8 is possible.

Mode of operation of geothermal heat pumps

In the cooling mode a GHP is transformed into a refrigerator. Water circulating in the earth loop is warmer than the surrounding ground. It therefore releases heat to the ground, cooling in the process. The cooled water then passes through a heat exchanger in the heat pump. Within the heat exchanger refrigerant, gas heated by a compressor releases its heat to the water, which then begins its travel to release heat to the ground. The refrigerant, having released its heat energy, becomes a cold gas after passing through an expansion valve which is used to cool air or water. In a ducted air system the heat pump's fan circulates warm air from the building through the coils containing the cold refrigerant. The resultant cooled air is then blown through the ductwork of the building. The cold refrigerant in the air coil picks up heat energy from the building and then travels to the compressor where it again becomes a hot gas and the cycle starts again.

A reversing valve linked to the compressor enables the heat pump to revert to a heating mode. In this case the water in the earth loop is colder than the surrounding ground and draws warmth from it. This heat is conveyed to the heat exchanger in the heat pump where the refrigerant absorbs heat from the water. The water leaves the heat exchanger to circulate through the earth and pick up more heat. The refrigerant, now converted to a gas having absorbed the heat from the earth loop, travels from the heat exchanger to the compressor. After compression the temperature of the refrigerant rises to about 65°C. It then passes to the building's heating distribution system, which frequently comprises an underfloor hot water circuit.

After the refrigerant has released its heat it returns to the earth loop heat exchanger to start the cycle once more (see Fig. 4.3).

Whilst heat pump technology has proved popular in the USA it still has to establish itself in the UK. To help with this process a business park in Cornwall has just been completed that is exclusively heated by heat pumps supplied by Kensa Engineering of Falmouth. At present this is one of the few companies constructing heat pumps as opposed to importing them (see Fig. 4.4).

It is the Tolvaddon Energy Park which exploits geothermal energy with nineteen heat pumps which pump water around boreholes to a depth of 70 m. The existence of this project is due to the support of the Regional Development Agency (RDA) for the South West and its insistence on the use of geothermal energy. The heat pumps were supplied by Kensa Engineering.

Air-sourced air heat pumps

Instead of drawing warmth or coolth from a ground or water source, in warmer climes it is possible for the external source to be the air. In cooling mode the compressor pumps refrigerant to the outside coil where it condenses into a liquid. The air flowing across the coil removes heat from the refrigerant. It is then transported to the inside coil where it picks up heat from the interior of the building. Internal air is blown across the inside coil where the liquid refrigerant evaporates giving up heat in the process. This cool air is blown into the building.

To provide heating the reversing valve in the pump directs refrigerant to the inside coil first. This makes the inside coil the condenser, releasing heat to the interior duct system. The outside coil becomes the evaporator, collecting heat from the ambient air.

Air-source heat pumps are becoming increasingly efficient. In fact, milder winters in the UK mean that inverter-speed-controlled compressors make air-source heat pumps more efficient than ground-source heat pumps. This version of the heat pump is mainly used to serve ducted air systems; there are very few available which operate wet underfloor heating systems. However, due to the absence of extensive external works, air-source heat pumps are much cheaper than ground-source systems.

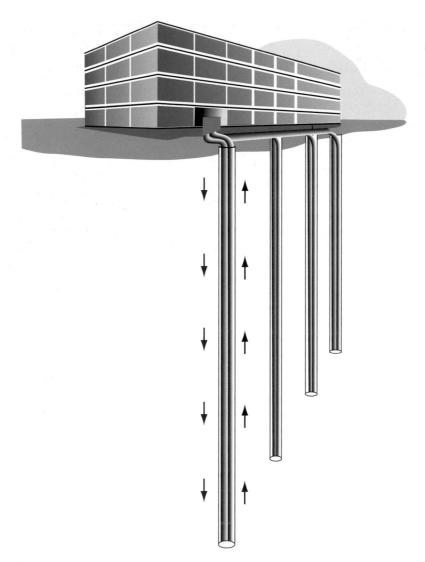

Figure 4.3   Ground source heat pumps in a commercial building context (source: Geoscience)

Variations

Rather than using electricity to power the compressor and fans, there is the prospect that natural gas or biofuel could be used to heat a Stirling engine to work the compressor and generate electricity for the fans. The excess heat could heat the building or provide domestic hot water.

There is also potential for heat from natural gas or biogas to supplement the output from the heat pump when the external temperature falls below 1.6°C. Such dual-fuel systems will be particularly attractive where gas prices are significantly lower than electricity costs.

Sustainability

In certain locations the geothermal heat pump can reduce energy consumption and therefore CO_2 emissions by up to 72% compared with electric central heating and standard air conditioning equipment.

Figure 4.4 Heat pump assembly at Kensa works

Where ground-coupled heat pumps are connected to the grid, given the present fuel mix across the EU, this results in a 40% reduction in CO_2 emissions compared with modern fossil fuel alternatives. Add to this the fact that a ground loop lasts in excess of 50 years and the fact that heat pumps have high reliability and require no routine maintenance, the sustainability credentials of the technology are impressive.

Economics

In terms of capital cost it is still the case that heat pumps are at a disadvantage compared with fossil fuel technologies. For example, the cost of a ground-source heat pump in the UK is at present 2 to 3 times that of a conventional fossil fuel boiler. In the case of a resistive electric installation like electric underfloor heating the cost disparity is even greater. It is in running costs that the advantages are to be found. In more recently built well-insulated homes with good thermal mass in the UK it is possible to achieve revenue savings as compared with mains gas, especially when maintenance costs are factored in.

Things are better in the commercial sector. Where new low-energy buildings need both heating and cooling it is possible to demonstrate that ground-source heat pumps are competitive with conventional systems. This is because of cost savings in terms of reduced plant room area, absence of fuel tanks, flues and gas connection. Capitalized running cost benefits also help to tip the balance in favour of heat pumps.

Examples

Four elementary schools in Lincoln, Nebraska USA installed geothermal heat pumps in 1996. In the first year of operation heating and cooling costs were $144,000 less than would have been incurred by conventional heating and cooling. In two other schools the total energy cost saving was 57%.

One of the most ambitious heat pump systems was installed in 1997 by Oslo International Airport. It uses a ground water reservoir both for heat storage and a heat medium for the heat pumps and employs a circulating water rather than a closed-loop system. The installation has seven large piston compressors and uses ammonia as the cooling agent. In summer it provides a district cooling network which can reduce the temperature by 10°C compared with the external temperature. The total cooling capacity is 8.8 MW using 630 m^3 per hour of circulating water.

In heating mode, 3 km of plastic pipe connect the energy centre with 18 wells, nine warm and nine cold. Water pumped from the warm to the cold wells works as a heat pump, providing a temperature difference of 26°C, equivalent to 8 MW of heat.

There are numerous advantages to heat pump technology which can be summarized as follows:

- It offers both heating and cooling.
- It is environment friendly and could be zero carbon coupled to a renewable source of electricity such as PVs used to charge batteries to run the pumps. However, it would need a substantial PV array to produce at least 3 kW of electricity needed to power a heat pump.
- It is efficient (relatively high coefficient of performance) and uses less energy than conventional central heating and cooling systems to maintain indoor comfort conditions.
- Maintenance costs are virtually zero.
- It is versatile and can provide different zonal temperatures simultaneously and can, for example, move heat from computer rooms to perimeter rooms requiring extra heating.
- Because it has relatively few moving parts it is a highly durable technology.
- It is quiet in operation.
- It can easily be retrofitted provided there already exists a low-temperature heating distribution system such as wet underfloor circuits. There is a problem for domestic retrofit in that homes in the UK normally have single-phase 230 V, 50 Hz electricity supply. This limits the compressor size to 3 kW which in turn limits the heat pump capacity. Above this capacity heat pumps need a three-phase supply which, in the UK domestic market, would necessitate soft start electric motors or an inverter.
- With underfloor wet systems the concrete floor slab insulated on the underside can act as a thermal store, enabling the heat pump to operate mainly on off-peak electricity.
- The heat output of a heat pump is purely conditioned by the size of the compressor.

With an accelerating demand for new housing in England, there is an ideal opportunity to exploit GHPs or water-sourced heat pumps on an ambitious scale. Whilst the technology is generally more expensive to install than conventional heating systems, the payback time can be as little as two years with the bonus that maintenance costs are lower (US Department of Energy). They could be used to serve groups of houses or individually installed. A grouped scheme could have a single twin-bore groundsource serving heat pumps in each house.

In the UK recent government initiatives such as the Warm Homes Programme and the promotion of micro-generation has given new impetus to GSHPs. This has been helped by the relentless rise in the price of oil and gas. According to Robin Curtis of Geoscience there is a 50% year on year growth in the installation of systems. This company alone is retrofitting one property per day. Penwith Housing Association in Penzance, UK, has pioneered the retrofitting of GSHPs in their older properties.

As energy problems become more acute, major boiler manufacturing companies such as Dimplex and Baxi are showing increasing interest in switching to heat pumps. Heat pumps are particularly appropriate for premises which need to dump heat, such as offices, hotels, restaurants etc. In such circumstances payback time can be less than five years.

One difficulty with this technology is that it has an image problem. It is often perceived as a version of air conditioning with all the environmental deficits which that implies.

Research is urgently needed into a standardized method of measuring the performance of heat pumps. Also there needs to be a cost-benefit analysis conducted across a wide range of samples across the EU. We need to ask why heat pumps are much more in evidence in Sweden with its lower temperatures than in the UK.

Since the publication of the first edition of this book, government action like the Affordable Warmth legislation and the Decent Homes Standard has given a boost to GSHPs in the social housing sector. In April 2006 the power company Powergen/Eon launched a system called 'HeatPlant', mainly for the social housing market. The package comprises a small GSHP system made by Calorex in either 3.5 or 5.0 kW mode which delivers hot water at over 65°C which meets a condition for funding laid down by the power Regulator Ofgen. Penwith Housing Association was the first to retrofit 14 homes in Cornwall, which has been a noted success.[2] This has generated considerable interest in both the retrofit and new build markets, including new homes for the Metropolitan Housing Trust in Nottingham. Another stimulus has come from the Mayor of London, who has required that all new developments over a certain area should derive 10% of their energy from renewables.

Increasingly the technology is being selected for public sector buildings like schools, health centres, community centres as well as offices. Geoscience based in Cornwall is currently consultant for a hospital project in the 2–3 MW range.[3]

Notes

1. Data from J. W. Lund and D. H. Freeston (2001), Worldwide direct use of geothermal energy 2000, *Geothermics* **30**(1), 29–68
2. See Smith, P. (2005), *Architecture in a Climate of Change,* 2nd edition, Architectural Press, Oxford, pp. 122–124
3. I am indebted to Dr Robin Curtis of Geoscience for these data

5 Wind power

The first known windmills were developed in Persia between 500 and 900 AD to pump water and grind grain. They consisted of vertical sails rotating round a central shaft. The first documented example of the technology in Europe dates from 1270. It shows a horizontal-axis machine mounted on a central post with four sails, known predictably as a 'postmill' machine. It took until the nineteenth century for the windmill sails to achieve peak efficiency. These sails had some of the crucial features which helped in the design of present-day turbine blades.

Energy consultants BTM produced a report in 2005[1] *International World Energy Development – Word Market Update 2004*. It showed that, on the world scale, 2004 saw 8154 MW of new installed capacity bringing the global total capacity to nearly 48 GW. This represents an increase of 20%. Over the years 2000–2005 growth has averaged 15.8% per year. Europe accounted for 74% of the total in 2004. In that year Spain was the leading market with 2064 MW replacing Germany as the leader with its 2054 MW. Growth stalled in the Americas in 2004 with only 516 MW as against 1818 MW in 2003. The report predicts that, as a result of the Kyoto ratification, there will be increasing world interest in wind power. Assuming that the manufacturing base keeps pace with demand, annual installation could reach 29 GW by 2014 with a total accumulated capacity of 235 GW.

China increased its capacity from 98 MW to 198 MW over the same period. It plans to builds its first offshore project in the Bohai Sea off the northern province of Hebei. It will generate 1000 MW when completed in 2020. The first phase will be installed in 2007 generating 50 MW. The Chinese government claims the country has the potential to generate 250 GW from wind energy. So far only a tiny fraction of this capacity has been exploited.

Even more optimistic is the EWEA in its Windforce 12 plan which demonstrates how up to 12% of global electricity demand could be met by wind power by 2020. Time will tell.[2]

Compared with other renewable energy technologies, wind energy is the closest to being competitive with fossil-based systems. The technology is mature and robust, with offshore installations set to take off in Europe. These facts should dispel any uncertainty about the future role of wind in the energy scenarios of the twenty-first century.

This chapter is mainly concerned with small-scale wind generation which can operate as embedded generation in buildings and this is where some of the most interesting developments have taken place. In this context 'small' means wind machines that are scaled from a few watts to 20 kW. Machines between 1 and 5 kW may be used to provide either direct current

(DC) or alternating current (AC). They are mainly confined to the domestic level and are often used to charge batteries. The larger machines are suitable for commercial/industrial buildings and groups of houses.

Small-scale electricity production on site has economic disadvantages in the UK given the present buy-in rates for small operators. Currently the government is considering how to redress this inequity and thereby give a substantial boost to the market for small-scale renewables. Wind generation will do well if this happens since it is much less expensive in terms of installed cost per kilowatt than PV, which makes it an attractive proposition as a building-integrated power source.

Wind patterns in the built environment are complex as the air passes over, around and between buildings. Accordingly a wind generator introduced into this environment must be able to cope with high turbulence caused by buildings. Such conditions tend to favour vertical-axis machines as opposed to the horizontal versions which have proliferated in wind farms. This is because the vertical versions may be able to operate at lower wind speeds and they are less stressed mechanically by turbulence. In addition, horizontal-axis machines mounted on roofs tend to transmit vibrations through the structure of the buildings. Because of the bending moment produced by the tower under wind load, measures must be taken to provide adequate strength in the building structure. This is not easily achieved in retrofit situations.

By their very nature the vertical-axis machines are not affected by changes in wind direction or turbulence. They can be sited on roofs or walls. They have been particularly successful mounted on the sides of oil platforms in the North Sea (see Fig. 5.1).

The machines are well balanced, transmitting minimum vibration and bending stress to walls or roofs. They also have a high output power-to-weight ratio. A further advantage is that the electricity generator is located beneath the rotors and therefore can be located within the envelope of the building.

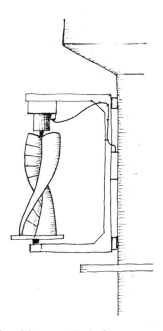

Figure 5.1   Helical side mounted turbine on oil platform

Wind generation can be complemented by PVs by the system patented by Altechnica (see the section Building integrated systems, p. 60). The wind generators continue operating at night when PVs are in retirement.

A projection in *WIND Directions,* March 2001, estimated that the global market for small turbines by 2005 would be around €173 million and several hundreds of millions by 2010. For example, in the Netherlands alone there is the potential for 20,000 urban turbines to be installed on industrial and commercial buildings by 2011.

The increasing deregulation of the energy market creates an increasingly attractive proposition for independent off-grid small-scale generation, insulating the operator from price fluctuations and reliability uncertainties, with the proviso that there is a level playing field.

Currently there are several versions of vertical-axis machines on the market. However, they are still undergoing development. When it is fully appreciated that these machines are reliable, silent, low maintenance, easy to install and competitive on price, it is likely the market will expand rapidly. At present the regulatory regime for small turbines is much less onerous than for >20 kW machines. It is to be hoped that the bureaucrats fail to spot this red tape opportunity.

Research conducted by Delft University of Technology and Ecofys identified five building conditions to determine their effectiveness for wind turbines. Four are described as 'wind catchers', 'wind collectors', 'wind sharers' and 'wind gatherers', terms which define their effect on wind speed. The wind catcher is well suited to small turbines, being usually high and benefiting from a relatively free wind flow. Small horizontal-axis machines could be satisfactory in this situation.

The wind collector type of building has a lower profile and can be subject to turbulence. This is where the vertical-axis machine comes into its own. The third type, wind sharers, are found in industrial areas and business parks. Their relatively even roof height and spaced-out siting makes such buildings subject to high winds and turbulence. Ecofys has produced a diagram which depicts how four urban situations cope with varying wind conditions. There is a fifth category, the 'wind dreamer', which relates to low-rise developments (see Fig. 5.2).

Development work is continuing on designs for turbines which are suitable for the difficult wind conditions found in urban situations. This is appropriate since climate change predictions indicate that wind speeds will increase as the atmosphere heats up and so becomes more dynamic. There is growing confidence that there will be a large market for mini-turbines in various configurations on offices, housing blocks and individual dwellings.

Types of small-scale wind turbine

Most small systems have a direct-drive permanent-magnet generator which limits mechanical transmission losses. Systems under 2 kW usually have a 24–48 V capacity aimed at battery charging or a DC circuit rather than having grid compatibility.

Up to the present, horizontal-axis machines are much more in evidence than the vertical-axis type, even at this scale. These machines have efficient braking systems for when wind speed is excessive. Some even tip backwards in high winds, adopting the so-called 'helicopter position'. There are advantages to horizontal-axis machines such as:

- the cost benefit due to economy of scale of production
- it is a robust and tested technology
- automatic start-up
- high output.

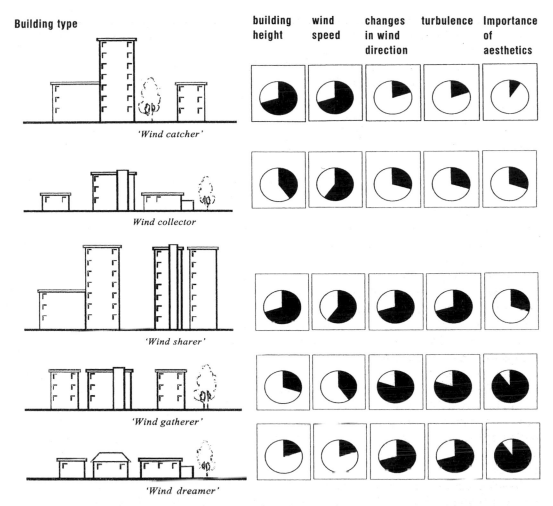

Figure 5.2   Categories of building cluster and their effectiveness for wind generation (courtesy Ecofys and *REW*)

The disadvantages are:

- the necessity of a high mast
- mounted on buildings they require substantial foundation support
- in urban situations where there can be large variations in wind direction and speed, this necessitates frequent changes of orientation and blade speed – this not only undermines power output it also increases the dynamic loading on the machine with consequent wear and tear
- there are noise problems with this kind of machine, especially associated with braking in high winds
- they can be visually intrusive.

As stated earlier, vertical-axis turbines are particularly suited to urban situations and to being integrated into buildings. They are discrete and virtually silent and much less likely to trigger

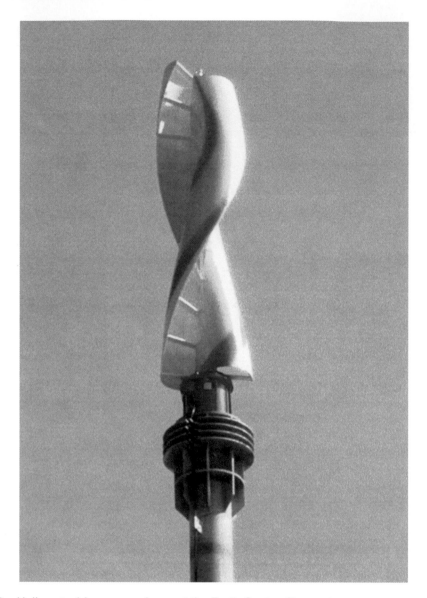

Figure 5.3   Helican turbine on a column at the Earth Centre, Doncaster

the wrath of planning officials. This type has even been the basis for an art work as in a sports stadium at Yurigoaka, Japan.

A problem with some very small vertical-axis machines is that they need mechanical start-up, which can be achieved either by an electric motor or a link to a Savonius type rotor. The most common vertical-axis machine is the helical turbine as seen at the former Earth Centre, Doncaster (see Fig. 5.3). In that instance it is mounted on a tower but it can also be side-hung on a building.

Another variety is the S-Rotor which has an S-shaped blade (see Fig. 5.4).

The Darrieus-Rotor employs three slender elliptical blades which can be assisted by a wind deflector. This is an elegant machine which nevertheless needs start-up assistance.

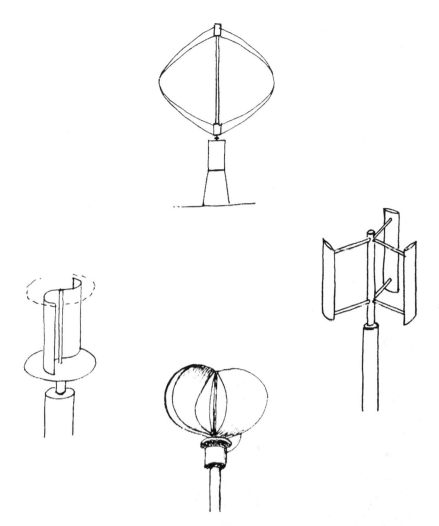

Figure 5.4 Left: S-Rotor; top centre: Darrieus-Rotor; bottom centre: Lange turbine; right: H-Darrieus-Rotor

A variation of the genre is the H-Darrieus-Rotor with triple vertical blades extending from the central axis. Yet another configuration is the Lange turbine which has three sail-like wind scoops (see Fig. 5.4). Last in this group is the 'spiral flugel' turbine in which twin blades create, as the name indicates, a spiral partnership (see Fig. 5.5).

Returning to the horizontal-axis machines, a development from the 1970s has placed the turbine blades inside an aerofoil cowling. A prototype developed at the University of Rijeka, Croatia, claims that this combination can produce electricity 60% more of the time compared with conventional machines. This is because the aerofoil concentrator enables the machines to produce electricity at slower wind speeds than is possible with conventional turbines.

The cross-section of the cowling has a profile similar to the wing of an aircraft, which creates an area of low pressure inside the cowling. This has the effect of accelerating the air over the turbine blades. As a result, more electricity is produced for a given wind speed as well as generating at low air speeds. This amplification of wind speed has its hazards in that blades

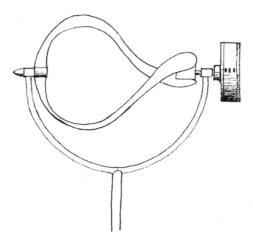

Figure 5.5   Spiral Flugel rotor

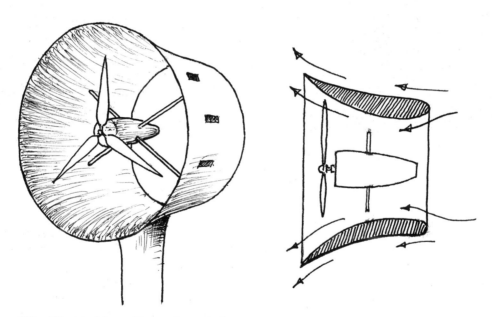

Figure 5.6   Wind turbine with cowling wind concentrator

can be damaged. The answer has been to introduce hydraulically driven air release vents into the cowling, which are activated when the pressure within the cowling is too great. They also serve to stabilize electricity output in turbulent wind conditions, which makes them appropriate for urban sites.

This technology can generate power from 1 kW to megawatt capacity. It is being considered for offshore application. The device is about 75% more expensive than conventional rotors but the efficiency of performance is improved by a factor of five as against a conventional horizontal-axis turbine (see Fig. 5.6).

Figure 5.7 'Aeolian' roof devised by Altechnica

Building integrated systems

There is increasing interest in the way that the design of buildings can incorporate renewable technologies including wind turbines. Up to now such machines have been regarded as an adjunct to buildings but a concept patented by Altechnica of Milton Keynes demonstrates how multiple turbines can become a feature of the design.

The system is designed to be mounted on the ridge of a roof or at the apex of a curved roof section. Rotors are incorporated in a cage-like structure which is capped with an aerofoil wind concentrator called in this case a 'solairfoil'. The flat top of the solairfoil can accommodate PVs. Where the rotors are mounted at the apex of a curved roof, the effect is to concentrate the wind in a manner similar to the Croatian cowling (see Fig. 5.7).

The advantage of this system is that it does not become an over-assertive visual feature and is perceived as an integral design element. It is also a system which can easily be fitted to existing buildings where the wind regime is appropriate. Furthermore it indicates a building which is discretely capturing the elements and working for a living. Altechnica has also illustrated how small scale rotors can be incorporated into the design of a high building. This approach has been demonstrated by Bill Dunster Architects in their SkyZed concept.

This is a multi-storey residential block consisting of four lobes which, on plan, resemble the petals of a flower, hence its colloquial name the 'flower-tower'. The curved floor plates serve to accelerate the wind by up to a factor of four at the core of the building. Here vertical-axis generators are positioned at every fourth floor. This is the only type of turbine appropriate for

Figure 5.8   Flying Electric Generator system (courtesy of Sky Windpower Corporation; artist, Ben Shepherd)

this situation, being virtually silent in operation. Also at every fourth floor there are access platforms linking the accommodation lobes and serving as platforms to view the rotors. This building will be considered in more detail as a case study (see Figs 15.11 and 15.12 on pp. 155–6 and also www.zedfactory.com).

One of the most ambitious wind projects has emerged from Australia with the idea of a power station in the sky. High-altitude winds have high velocity and are constant. The idea is to install flying wind generators at 15,000 feet to harvest this energy. 'High altitude wind power represents the most concentrated flux of renewable energy found on Earth'. Depending on location, flying generators could be 90% efficient, which is well over three times that of onshore counterparts. Bryan Roberts, Professor of Engineering at the University of Technology, Sydney, has teamed up with Sky Windpower of San Diego, which has approval to conduct tests over the California desert. GPS technology will keep the turbines stable in space. The system is rated at 240 kW rotor diameters of 35 feet. The system will use existing rotor technology but also benefit from very strong but lightweight tether ropes. Even stronger strength to weight ratio materials are being developed. The device would clearly pose a hazard to aircraft. Its inventors claim that airspace restricted for these turbines would be less than that already restricted for civil aviation use. Military aircraft are another matter. If employed in mass the makers claim a cost of less than 2 cents (US) per kilowatt hour, taking account of life cycle costs.

A Canadian company, Magenn Power Inc., has also developed an airborne tethered wind rotor system (see Fig. 5.9). Horizontal-axis blades rotate around a helium-filled cylinder at heights up to 300 metres (1000 feet). Power is transmitted down the tether to a transformer on the ground which feeds into the electricity grid. The 'Magnus effect' (the effect of the aerodynamic forces on a cylinder) of the rotation provides extra lift whilst keeping the device stable within a restricted location. The company claims that it can operate at wind speeds between 1 and over 28 metres per second. It has a load factor of 40–50%, placing it well ahead of conventional wind turbines.

In addition to its efficiency and low installed cost per watt, the system has several advantages:

- clusters of machines can be sited close to high concentrations of demand, greatly reducing transmission losses and costs
- it can reach altitudes at which winds are stronger and more constant than is possible with fixed turbines
- maintenance is straightforward and easily performed
- it is portable and can easily be moved to sites with more favourable wind conditions
- it can provide rapid access to power in emergency or disaster situations where grid power is not available
- it offers a reliable source of cheap energy for remote locations in developing countries where grid power will probably never be available. It can afford near-continuity of supply in conjunction with solar and possibly micro-hydropower
- technically the system can be scaled up to very large units which can supplement an established grid in large urban areas.

A domestic scale 4 kW version was due to be marketed from early 2006. The company is confident that the system can produce electricity cheaper than any other wind system. The installed cost is estimated at £7000. See Figure 5.10.

Finally the subject of wind power cannot be left without reference to changes in distribution technology which are likely to come increasingly in evidence as offshore wind farms are developed at ever greater distances from land. It concerns transporting electricity as medium to high-voltage DC current instead of the conventional AC. As distances from the shore increase from the present 5–15 km to 50–200 km, AC cables become increasingly inefficient. At a distance of 100 km, AC cables use so much electricity generating heat that at the destination there is virtually no usable power. The principle is that the AC current generated by the turbines is converted to high-voltage DC for transportation and then back to AC in a conversion terminal onshore. By changing to DC transportation the theoretical transport capacity of existing lines could be increased by a factor of two. This switch has been made economic by the introduction of DC transformers, powerful switches and custom-developed safety and protection devices.

This DC conversion technology offers great advantages in urban situations whenever it becomes necessary to enlarge the capacity of the existing grid. Medium-voltage DC (MVDC) technology involves raising the cable voltage and this can be done with existing AC cables without having to expose the cables. Thus the curse of all urban dwellers, the digging up of roads, could be considerably curtailed.

The European Commission White Paper on Renewable Sources of Energy set a goal of 12% penetration of renewables across the EU by 2010. Within this target the goal for wind energy is 40 GW of installed power producing 8 TWh of electricity. This would save 72 million tonnes of CO_2 per year. The European wind Energy Association considers this to be conservative

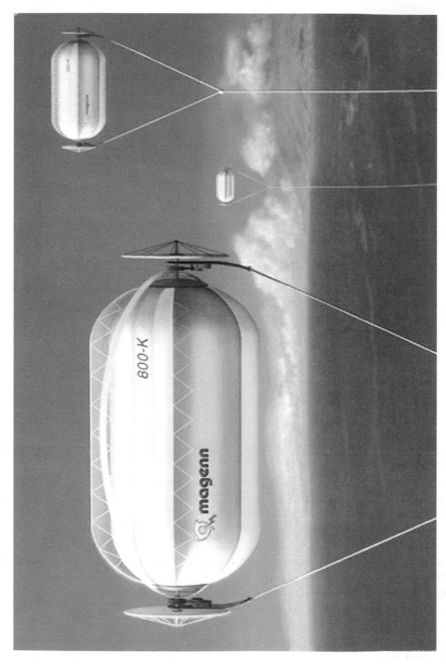

Figure 5.9   Magenn airborne tethered wind turbines (courtesy of Magenn Power Inc.)

Figure 5.10 Magenn tethered 4 kW system (courtesy of Magenn Power Inc.)

since current growth rates suggest that a target of 60 GW is feasible. That would mean that by 2020 wind would account for almost 10% of all EU electricity production.

Another important statistic is that the latest version of a 600 kW turbine will save between 20,000 and 36,000 tonnes of CO_2 over its 20-year life. The difference is due to varying site and wind conditions. As yet the cost benefit of such a technology in terms of avoided damage to the biosphere, human health, plant damage etc., is not acknowledged in the price regime. However, the European Union Extern-E study has sought to put a price on the damage inflicted by fossil fuels compared with wind energy. The research has concluded that, for 40 GW of wind power installed by 2010, and with a total investment of €24.8 billion up to 2010, CO_2 emissions could be reduced by 54 million tonnes per year in the final year. The cumulative saving would amount to 320 million tonnes of CO_2, giving avoided external costs of up to €15 billion.

This is the first sign of a revolution in the way of accounting for energy. When the avoided costs of external damage are realistically factored-in to the cost of fossil fuels, the market should have no difficulty in switching to renewable energy *en masse*.

During 2005 there was increasing interest in mounting small turbines on the roofs of buildings. The domestic market was particularly targeted with attractive claims regarding their energy production (see Fig. 5.11).

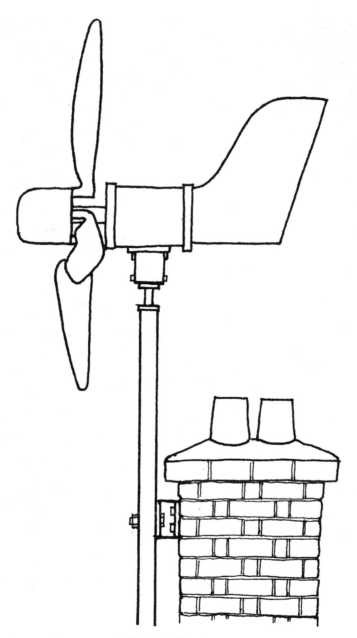

Figure 5.11   Rooftop turbine around 750 W by Windsave

Nick Martin of the Hockerton Housing Project,[2] which has building-integrated PVs and two free-standing wind turbines, is sceptical about some of the claims being made for these micro-wind machines. He warns that the gap between the claims and the reality reflects badly on the whole industry.[3] Micro-turbines should perhaps carry a pay-back time health warning. In the Hockerton Project there are four earth-sheltered houses built to superinsulation standards. Two 5 kW wind turbines and a PV array are enough to ensure that the homes are net zero CO_2 and their energy demand is about one tenth that of an average home.

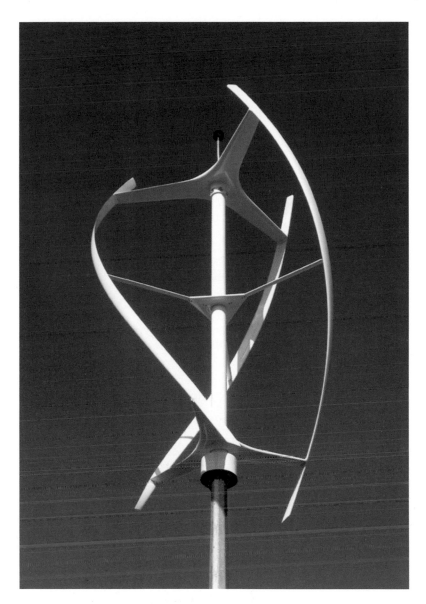

Figure 5.12 Triple helix vertical axis quietrevolution wind generator (courtesy of quietrevolution ltd.)

Nick Martin's concerns should be allayed by an elegant triple-helix vertical-axis quietrevolution wind turbine ideal for urban situations produced by energy consultancy XCO_2 (see Fig. 5.12). It is rated at 6 kW, producing ~10,000 kW hours per year at average wind speeds. Free-standing, it is around 14 m high with a swept area of 3 m. Mounted above buildings, its height is 8 m. This machine promises to represent a breakthrough in aesthetically pleasing and cost-effective compact wind generators, which should be attractive to business and housing developers.

Notes

1. Data from the 'World Market Update 2000 Report' from BTM Consult which produces statistics on an annual basis
2. The Hockerton Housing project is described in Smith, P. (2005) *Architecture in a Climate of Change,* 2nd edn, Architectural Press, Oxford, pp. 93–95
3. See *Building for a Future,* Nick Martin, Vol. 15, No. 3, Winter 2005–6

6 Photovoltaic cells

Electricity is produced from solar energy when photons or particles of light are absorbed by semiconductors. This is the basis of the photovoltaic (PV) cell. Most solar cells in current use are built from solid-state semiconducting material. Semiconductors are at the centre of the electronic revolution of the last century and it is worth a moment to consider how they function.

Silicon is a typical semiconductor material in that its electrical properties can be influenced in a number of ways. The electronic structure of a solid, that is, the disposition of its electrons, falls into bands separated by 'band gaps'. A flow of electrons represents an electric current. The ability of electrons to move is determined by the extent to which a particular band is filled. Electrons in filled bands are relatively static. So solids with fully filled bands cannot conduct electricity – there is no space to allow electrons to move. Such materials are insulators. Materials with partially filled bands like most metals are conductors.

In all solids the saturated electronic band that has the highest energy density is called the 'valence band'. The next band above the valence band is the 'conduction band'. In insulators this band is empty; in metals, partially filled. The electronic band structure of silicon is similar to that of insulators. The valence band is completely filled and the conduction band empty. What distinguished a semiconductor from a pure insulator is the size of the band gap. In silicon it is small enough for a few electrons in the valence band to pick up enough thermal energy to hop into the conduction band where they have the space to move. This leaves a vacancy or hole in the valence band which has a real existence with an electrical charge opposite to that of an electron. It is, in effect, a virtual particle. So, in silicon, an electrical current is carried by a few energetic particles in the conduction band moving in one direction and by positively charged 'holes' in the valence bands moving in the opposite direction. This movement of particles is activated by the application of heat. The charged particles are thermally excited.

The conductivity of semiconductors can be improved by the addition of certain foreign atoms that provide extra charge carriers. These atoms are called 'dopants'. In the case of silicon an atom of arsenic replacing an atom of silicon results in the material acquiring an extra electron. The valence band being full means that this extra electron sits within the band gap which in turn means that it takes less energy to enable it to gravitate to the conduction band. In other words it more readily becomes a thermally excited charge carrier. This kind of doping introduces negative charge carriers, hence its description 'n-type' doping.

Conversely, using a dopant that has one fewer valence electrons than silicon creates a hole in the valence band. This hole behaves as a positive charge carrier. This is described as p-type doping. This manipulation of the electronic properties of silicon by doping has provided the basis of silicon microelectronics. At the heart of this technology is the so-called p-n junction or interface.

In the case of photovoltaic cells a layer of semiconductor material lies back to back with another semiconductor. One is p-doped and the other n-doped. This sets up an electrical field at the interface. When light falls on the cell, the energy from the photons frees some electrons in the semiconductors which are propelled to the extremities of the two-layer structure. This creates a difference in potential which generates an electrical current. Metal electrodes are attached to the two faces of the cell to complete an electrical circuit (see Fig. 6.1).

At present in most cells the p-doped and n-doped cells are formed within a monolithic piece of crystalline silicon. To reduce efficiency loss through reflection, most crystalline cells are chemically etched to roughen the surface. The absorption bandwidth of these cells is from 350 nm, the ultraviolet part of the spectrum, to the near-infrared 1.1 μm. The fundamental conversion efficiency limit of crystalline silicon is said to be 29%.

A characteristic of such cells is that heat is generated when electrons are propelled to the boundary of the n-doped semiconductor, heat which needs to be dissipated, otherwise the efficiency of the cell is reduced.

Amorphous silicon cells

Less efficient but cheaper to produce are silicon-based cells which do not have a crystalline atomic structure. Hydrogenated amorphous silicon (a-Si:H) comprising a thin film 0.5 μm thick form the basis of highly light-absorbent cells, hence the description 'thin film solar cell'. They are produced by atomic deposition over a large area and consequently much more economical to produce than crystalline silicon cells which involve slicing up slabs of crystalline silicon grown by a slow crystallization process.

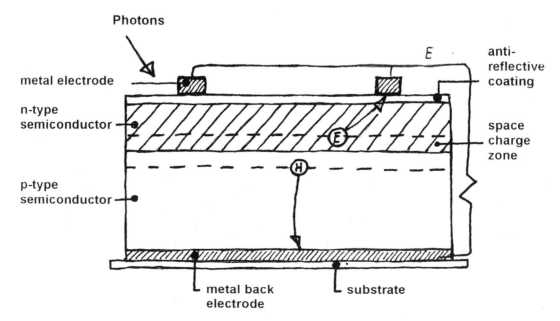

Figure 6.1   Crystalline silicon photovoltaic cell

The efficiency of this technology has been improved by stacking cells which capture light at different wavelengths. Different alloys of silicon capture the blue, green and red/infrared parts of the spectrum. A triple junction terrestrial concentrator solar cell has been produced by Spectrolab Inc of the USA which has achieved an efficiency in the laboratory of 34%. The variations in the silicon are:

- Top: amorphous silicon alloy (a-Si alloy) – blue
- Middle: a-Si + 10% germanium – green
- Bottom: a-Si + 40–50% germanium – red/infrared.

Light passes through all three layers and is reflected back by a silver/zinc oxide reflector. The cells are able to withstand highly concentrated sunlight and using a concentrator reduces the number of cells needed to produce a given amount of electricity.

Dye-based cells

The dominance of silicon is being challenged by a new generation of solar cells that mimic the process of photosynthesis. Developed by Michael Gratzel and Brian O'Regan of the University of Lausanne, this cell uses a dye containing ruthenium ions that absorb visible light analogous to chlorophyll in nature. The dye is applied to nanocrystals of the semiconductor titanium dioxide or titania. The titania has the electronic property of being able to draw electrons from the ruthenium and propel them off into an electrical circuit.

The construction of the cell involves sandwiching a 10-μm-thick film of dye-coated titania between two transparent electrodes. The tightly packed nanocrystals form a porous film that maximizes the light-absorbing capacity of the cell. The space between the electrodes is filled with a liquid electrolyte containing iodine ions. These ions replace those knocked out of the dye by the action of the photons. The two electrodes are connected to form a circuit that carries the electrical discharge (see Fig. 6.2).

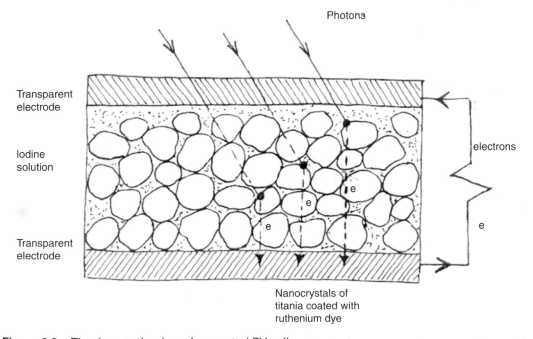

Figure 6.2 Titanium–ruthenium dye-coated PV cell

The conversion efficiency is around 10% in direct sunlight but up to 15% in the diffuse light of cloudy days, which makes these cells especially suitable for northern climes. The cost is claimed to be only 20% of the price of crystalline silicon, and may be even less since huge deposits of titanium have been discovered in Australia.

Solar cells which are transparent are the solution to the wider application of façade PVs. This means creating cells which can produce a significant amount of electricity by absorbing light only in the infrared end of the spectrum. These would be coated with a dye that is transparent yet absorbs light in this invisible part of the spectrum. Michael Gratzel of the University of Lausanne considers that such cells could achieve a conversion rate of 10%.

Monolithic tandem concentrator cells

The Fraunhofer Institute for Solar Energy in Freiburg has developed a PV based on a thin film structure of two semiconductors: gallium indium arsenide and gallium indium phosphide. Solar concentrators are incorporated in the cell which increases the solar intensity by factors ranging from 100 to 1000. Because the optical concentrators focus solar energy onto a small area, this reduces the area of cells required for a given output. In the laboratory the cells achieve an efficiency of 29% but values up to 35% are expected to result from further developments. The disadvantage of this technology is that the concentrators are really only efficient in sunlight.

Flexible solar panels

Shell Renewables and Akzo Nobel in the Netherlands are jointly developing a low-cost process for mass-producing flexible solar cell panels. A special semiconductor coating is applied to rolls of flexible foil substrate on an almost continuous basis. The process is being developed in parallel by the Technical Universities of Delft and Eindhoven, Utrecht University, the Energy Research Centre of the Netherlands, NOVEM the Dutch agency for energy and the environment and the European Union. This technology promises to be ideal for roof and wall panel application.

Other PV technologies include cadmium telluride (CdTe) cells being developed in the USA (BP Solar) and Germany (Siemens). First Solar in the USA has developed a 100 MW CdTe coating facility and a 25 MW module fabrication plant. The process deposits CdTe on glass with a transparent conducting oxide. Modules of $0.75\,m^2$ ($8\,ft^2$) will be produced by a plant commencing 2002. The efficiency is modest at 8% but, in compensation, the cost is low combined with the fact that it can be employed as roof and wall covering. The main disadvantage is that cadmium is a highly toxic metal.

The Boeing Corporation has developed a gallium arsenide thin film cell which can achieve high absorption rates. A single junction cell has realized 28.7% efficiency whilst a tandem two-junction cell has reached 33%.

Siemens has focused on a copper indium diselenide (CIS) cell with an efficiency of 9–11%.

An innovative technology has been developed by Daystar Inc. of Denver, Colorado. It employs 1 mm diameter filaments of polycrystalline copper indium gallium diselenide (CIGs) as a semiconductor deposited on stainless steel wires. Light is focused onto the wires by built-in elliptical lenses. The cost of materials is claimed to be one fifth that of silicon cells and peak efficiency is said to be 18% (www.daystartech.com/products.htm).

Plastic solar cells

Scientists at Siemens, Germany have developed a printed organic solar cell with an efficiency of 5%. In the present state of the art they expect this to reach 7%. If the cell is cheap enough in the market place, this will still be an attractive proposition especially where there is no constraint on the size of platform. The cost of electricity per kWh will still be substantially less than for conventional silicon PVs.

A further step has been taken by chemists at the University of California at Berkeley. They have developed a flexible solar cell that can be painted onto any surface. Their solar cell is a hybrid consisting of inorganic nanorods dispersed within an organic polymer or plastic. The nanorods are manufactured in a solution containing cadmium selenide to a diameter of around 7 nanometres (nm). These absorb sunlight. The nanorods are then mixed with a plastic semi-conductor to coat a transparent electrode to a thickness of 200 nm. The cell is completed with an aluminium coating to act as a back electrode.

The nanorods behave like wires able to absorb light of a particular wavelength. When subjected to light they generate an electron plus an electron hole. The electron travels the length of the rod to be collected by the aluminium electrode. The hole, which mimics an electron, is transferred to the plastic or hole carrier where it migrates to its electrode thereby creating a current.

At present hybrid solar cells based on nanorods and plastic semiconductors achieve an efficiency of 2%. However, there is confidence among the scientists that realizing an efficiency of 10% will only be a matter of time.

The researchers claim that using inorganic semiconductors coupled with organic polymers achieves the best of both worlds since polymers offer the advantage of processing at room temperature which is relatively low cost and permits the use of a flexible substrate. Inorganic semiconductors have well-established electronic properties well suited as solar cell material.

If efficiency can be raised to 10% this promises to revolutionize the PV industry, for example by incorporating light concentrators in the cell. A commercial solar cell might have three layers to absorb light across the spectrum of sunlight.

Researchers at the University of Toronto led by Edward Sargent have come up with a novel material which contains semi-conductor nanocrystals that respond to the infra-red end of the light spectrum. This enables them to produce more electricity *pro rata* than conventional solar cells. The cells are so small that they can be held in suspension in solution such as paint or dye. This gives the technology considerable potential, for example to be painted onto walls of buildings and incorporated into fabrics. These plastic solar cells are claimed to be cheap and amenable to mass production. The inventors are confident it will transform the PV industry within ten years.[1]

Scientists at Cambridge University are developing an organic cell which uses two different types of carbon molecule, which, when mixed together, separate into layers and start converting light to electricity. So far the device has achieved 34% efficiency but only in the blue-green part of the spectrum. The objective is to encompass the whole spectrum. This would seem to be a technology to watch.

Finally, one manufacturer, Nanosolar of Palo Alto, California, is developing 'next generation' solar cells based on ultra-thin light absorbers. The semi-conductor film will be ~10,000 times thinner than crystalline silicon cells and will be based on three-dimensional nanocomposite architecture. This will make it possible for the cells to absorb light from most wavelengths of the spectrum. In terms of material use and manufacture this technology promises to offer considerable savings compared with crystalline silicon, not least the capability of a bulk rolling manufacturing process. The company's chief executive claims that the cell can deliver a ten-fold improvement in the cost-to-performance ratio compared with crystalline silicon. Another important feature is that the cells last considerably longer than conventional cells – nearer to a lifetime than the 20 years of silicon-based PVs. They also do not degrade with exposure to the elements. These will be major considerations when it comes to selecting building-integrated systems. The company aims at volume production in 2007. By 2012 there are plans to introduce ultra-thin three-dimensional absorber cells. (www.nanosolar.com/thin-film.com.htm)

Photovoltaics: cost projections

Some governments have intervened to enable PVs to achieve economies of scale, notably Germany, the USA and Japan. A combination of subsidies, market growth and technical gains promises to deliver sharp reductions in cost. A tripling of annual production would bring PV prices down to the level of conventional power. It is likely that the domestic market will provide the impetus for this expansion. The key to success will be the production of roof and wall systems that compete with conventional materials.[2]

Projections of PV market penetration

A joint research project by the European Photovoltaic Industry Association (EPIA) and Greenpeace has produced an estimate of the development of PVs to 2020 and 2040.[3] The EPIA represents 52 of Europe's leading PV companies.

The report estimates that the output of PV will rise from the 280 MWp in 2000 to over 40,000 MWp in 2020, producing about 274 TWh worldwide. This would account for 30% of Africa's needs. This assumes that:

- the market development over recent years is maintained
- there are national and regional support programmes
- there are national targets for PV installations and manufacturing capacity
- suitable sites are available including roofs
- there is a growth in demand from areas not grid-connected.

The International Energy Agency predicts that world electricity demand by 2020 will be 26,000 TWh with an installed capacity of 195 GWp. About half the world would be grid-connected, mostly in the industrialized countries. Assuming 80% of demand will be from homes with an average demand of 3 kW serving 3 people, by 2020 the total generating their own electricity would be 82 million with 35 million in Europe being grid-connected.

In developing countries the capacity by 2020 is expected to be 30 GWp, of which 10 GW will be used for homes with an average demand of 50 Wp. This would amount to one million using PV.

The overall effect would be to reduce CO_2 emissions by 164 million tonnes at the same time creating an employment potential of 2 million jobs.

By 2040, assuming:

- a 15% p.a. growth in PV
- the lifetime of PVs of 20 years
- power consumption increasing from 26,000 TWh in 2020 to 35,000 TWh

then solar PV will account for 7368 TWh or 23% of world electricity output.

Photovoltaics and urban design

Towns and cities present an ideal opportunity for the exploitation of PVs. They have a high concentration of potential PV sites with a heavy energy demand. At the same time the physical infrastructure can support localized electricity generation. It is estimated that installing PVs on suitable walls and roofs could generate up to 25% of total demand.

It is worth noting that solar irradiation in Malmo, Sweden is higher than in southern England and only 20% less than Florence despite the difference in latitude. The biggest potential for PV is as systems embedded in buildings. It is expected that building integrated PV will account for 50% of the world PV installations by 2010, with the percentage being significantly higher in Europe.

The wide-scale adoption of PV in the urban environment will depend on the acceptance of the visual change it will bring about, especially in historic situations. There is still a barrier to be overcome and planning policy guidance may have to be amended to create a presumption in favour of retrofitting PVs to buildings.

The efficiency of PVs in a given location will depend on several factors such as:

- compact developments with fairly consistent roof heights are ideal for roof-mounted PVs
- orientation is an important factor
- a more open urban grain may exploit the potential of façade PVs. In this case overshading must be considered, especially in the context of seasonal changes in the sun's angle.

Nieuwland near Amersfoort in Holland is a new town in which building integrated PVs is a feature of many homes, producing a peak total of 1.3 MW (see Fig. 6.3).

A way of measuring the effectiveness of the urban massing to accommodate PV is the 'sky view factor' (SVF) devised by Koen Steemers and colleagues at the Martin Centre in the University of Cambridge. This gives an indication of the spacing between buildings and indicates the amount of the sky which is visible from any particular position in a city whether at

Figure 6.3   The new town of Nieuwland near Amersfoort (courtesy of Ecofys and *REW*)

Figure 6.4   Sky view factor for two towns: medieval Athens (left) and Grugliasco, Italy (source: The Martin Centre, Cambridge)

street or roof level. A totally unobstructed situation has a value of 1. Steemers gives two examples: a medieval part of Athens and Grugliasco in Italy. The average SVF from the streets for Athens is 0.68 and for Grugliasco, 0.82 (see Fig. 6.4).

The intensity of the grey indicates the degree of visible sky with white being the SVF of 1. In Athens the buildings are tightly packed at high density and so the streets offer few opportunities for façade building-integrated PVs (BIPVs). On the other hand, there is a relatively even overall building height which creates a good situation for roof PVs. The Italian example has a smaller overall area of roof but light shading at street level and therefore opportunities for façade BIPVs.

Surface-to-volume ratio

The surface area available for either façade or roof PV installation is largely determined by the surface-to-volume ratio. A high ratio of surface to volume suggests opportunities for façade-integrated PVs. However, in high-density situations, overshading will limit façade opportunities. On the other hand, lower values indicate opportunities for roof PVs. In the examples from Steemers the lighter the shading the more the PV opportunities. The lower the value the greater the potential for roof-mounted PVs (see Fig. 6.5).

As stated, the spacing between buildings is an important factor in determining façade PV opportunities. Figure 6.6 shows three plan orientations coupled with three height-to-width ratios. The street with west to east façades offers the least overall efficiency for solar access whereas the diagonal street offers the best overall solar opportunity. However, to sum up, wide spacing between buildings with a southerly aspect will be particularly suited to façade BIPV. Wide streets and city squares provide excellent opportunities for this PV mode. A tighter urban grain points to roof-mounted PVs.

The relationship between urban form and PV potential has been demonstrated by comparing four urban configurations all with a plot ratio of 1.7. Figure 6.7 shows how the percentage of façade area with annual irradiation of >800 kWh/m² varies with building type and location. The tower layout (pavilions) is the least efficient whereas the terraces offer the best exposure.

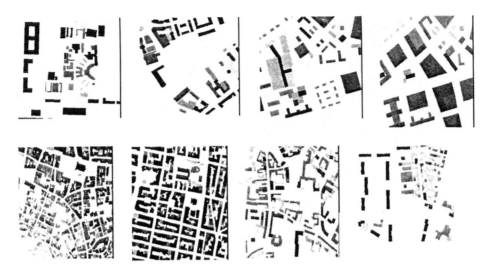

Figure 6.5 Comparative surface to volume ratios for European cities (source: The Martin Centre, Cambridge)

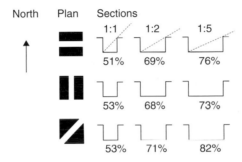

Figure 6.6 Solar access and space between buildings (source: The Martin Centre, Cambridge)

In conclusion, the suitability of BIPV is dependent upon a variety of factors. For example, flat roofs are the most appropriate sites in city centres, combining flexibility with unobtrusiveness.

In considering pitched roofs, the orientation, angle of tilt and aesthetic impact all have to be taken into account.

The suitability of PVs for integrating with buildings is dependent upon a variety of factors. For example, flat roofs are the most appropriate sites in city centres, combining flexibility with unobtrusiveness. In considering pitched roofs, the orientation, angle of tilt and aesthetic impact all have to be taken into account (see Fig. 6.8).

Figure 6.8 illustrates the efficiency of average PV cells at different angles and orientation. What is evident is that PV façades may make a significant solar contribution in combination with roof-mounted cells.

Reflected light is a useful supplemental form of energy for PVs. Many façades in city centres have high reflectance values offering significant levels of diffuse light for façade PVs on opposite elevations, thus making orientation less important. In glazed curtain wall buildings solar shading is now *de rigueur*. Here is a further opportunity to incorporate PVs into shading devices. When office blocks are refurbished the incorporation of PVs into a façade becomes highly cost-effective.

Urban area (plot ratio = 1.7)		Climate	Percentage of façade and annual irradiation c. 800 kW
Pavilion-Court		Athens	**30**
		Torino	17
		Fribourg	6
		Cambridge	2
		Tronheim	24
Pavilion		Athens	**13**
		Torino	4
		Fribourg	1
		Cambridge	6
		Tronheim	39
Slab		Athens	**39**
		Torino	23
		Fribourg	7
		Cambridge	2
		Tronheim	39
Terrace		Athens	**50**
		Torino	38
		Fribourg	11
		Cambridge	2
		Tronheim	14

Figure 6.7   Percentage of façade receiving solar radiation in four configurations (source: The Martin Centre, Cambridge)

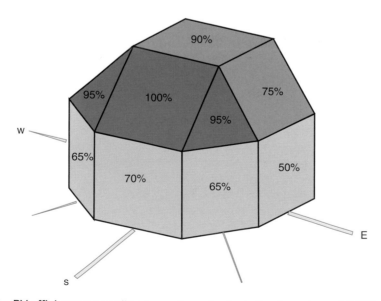

Figure 6.8   PV efficiency according to angle and orientation (courtesy of *REW*, p. 242, July–Aug 2005)

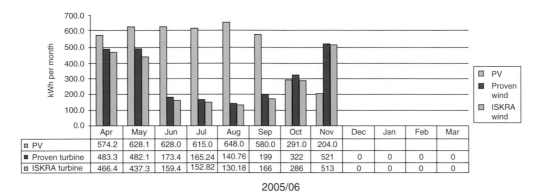

	Apr	May	Jun	Jul	Aug	Sep	Oct	Nov	Dec	Jan	Feb	Mar
▫ PV	574.2	628.1	628.0	615.0	648.0	580.0	291.0	204.0				
▪ Proven turbine	483.3	482.1	173.4	165.24	140.76	199	322	521	0	0	0	0
▫ ISKRA turbine	466.4	437.3	159.4	152.82	130.18	166	286	513	0	0	0	0

2005/06

Figure 6.9 Hockerton project analysis of output (HHP electricity production kWh per month) over 8 months from PV panels, Proven and ISKRA 5 kW turbines (courtesy of the Hockerton Housing Project)

In conservation areas there are particular sensitivities. The next generation of thin film PVs look like offering opportunities to integrate PVs into buildings without compromising their historic integrity.

As a postscript to Chapters 5 and 6 an assessment of the performance of two wind turbines and roof PVs offers a useful prediction of the electricity generation which can be expected from domestic scale installations (see Fig. 6.9). It is worth repeating that the four homes are net zero CO_2. Thus the scale of renewables on the site is of the order needed to meet the demands of houses that are 90% more energy-efficient than the average home if net zero CO_2 is to be achieved.

Notes

1. *New Scientist*, 23 January 1999, p. 40
2. See www.GreenMountain.com
3. *Solar Generation*

7 Fuel cells

It has taken since 1839, when Sir William Grove invented the technology, for the fuel cell to be recognized as the likely principal power source of the future. It is the fuel cell that will be the bridge between the hydrocarbon economy and hydrogen-based society. David Hart, who is head of fuel cells and hydrogen research at Imperial College London, has no doubt about the possibilities for fuel cells:

> *If fuel cells fulfil their potential, there's no reason why they shouldn't replace almost every battery and combustion engine in the world.*[1]

There is still considerable potential for improvements in the efficiency of fuel cells since they are not dependent upon heat *per se* but on electrochemical conversion which means they are not limited by the second law of thermodynamics.

Until recently one reason for scepticism about the technology was the cost. However, since 1989 there has been a dramatic fall in cost per kilowatt of output (see Fig. 7.1).

System developers are confident that cost will ultimately fall to $300–500 per kW installed capacity for stationary application, mostly due to economies of scale, but they are unable to predict a date.

In the USA there is considerable activity in fuel cell development, not least because of the DOE's (Department of Energy) upbeat stance over the technology.

> *The vision is staggering: a society powered almost entirely by hydrogen, the most abundant element in the universe. . . The overall goal of the DOE is to replace two to four quads of conventional energy with hydrogen by the year 2010, and replace 10 quads per year by 2030. A quad is the amount of energy consumed by one million households.*[2]

So, what is it about the fuel cell that gets people so excited?

Fuel cells are electrochemical devices that generate direct current (DC) electricity similar to batteries. Unlike batteries they require a continual input of a hydrogen-rich fuel. They have been described as electrochemical internal combustion engines. In essence the fuel cell is a reactor which combines hydrogen and oxygen to produce electricity, heat and water. It is a robust technology with no moving parts. It is clean, quiet and emits no pollution when fed directly with hydrogen.

At the outset it should be useful to provide a glossary of terms associated with this technology.

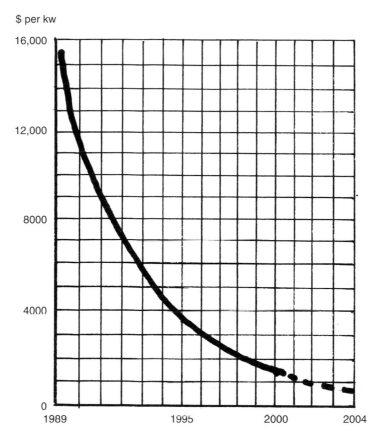

Figure 7.1 Improving economics of fuel cells (based on data from *New Scientist*, 25 November 2000)

Anode. Electrode at which an oxidation reaction takes place.

Bipolar plates. Plates used to connect fuel cells in series to form a stack and build up voltage. They can be made of steel, graphite or conducting polymer. The plates are designed to facili-tate gas distribution to each cell of the stack; to assist cooling; fluids separation and distri-bution; electrical conduction and physical support. Flow channels are carved into the plates to allow an even distribution of hydrogen and oxygen to the cells (see Fig. 7.3).

Catalyst. Molecule, metal or other chemical substance used to increase the rate of a reaction. The catalyst takes part in the reaction mechanism without being consumed by the reactants.

Cathode. Electrode at which a reduction reaction takes place.

Cogeneration. The utilization of both electrical and thermal energy from a power plant.

Electrode. Electric conductor through which a flow of electrons is created (an electrical cur-rent). An electrochemical system has a minimum of two: an anode and a cathode that are in direct contact with the electrolyte.

Electrolyte. A substance, solid or liquid, that conducts ions between electrodes in an electro-chemical cell. The electrolyte is in direct contact with the electrodes.

Energy density. The amount of available energy per unit weight or volume of the power plant.

Exothermic reaction. A chemical reaction that releases heat.

Ion exchange membrane. A thin film which allows ion conduction and separation of fuel (e.g. hydrogen) at the anode and oxidant (air) at the cathode. Another term for electrolyte.

Matrix. The electrolyte-containing layer between the anode and cathode of the fuel cell.

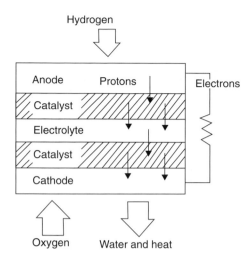

Figure 7.2   Polymer electrolyte or proton exchange membrane fuel cell

Polymer electrolyte membrane fuel cell

Generally fuel cells are classified by their electrolyte. One of the most common types of cell is the polymer electrolyte membrane fuel cell. Sometimes called the proton exchange membrane fuel cell (PEMFC in either case), it is also referred to as the solid polymer fuel cell. This is one of the most common types of cell, being appropriate for both vehicle and static application. Of all the cells in production it has the lowest operating temperature of 80°C. The cell consists of an anode and a cathode separated by an electrolyte, in this case usually Teflon. Both the anode and cathode are coated with platinum which acts as a catalyst. Hydrogen is fed to the anode and an oxidant (oxygen from the air) to the cathode. The catalyst on the anode causes the hydrogen to split into its constituent protons and electrons. The electrolyte membrane allows only protons to pass through to the cathode, setting up a charge separation in the process. The electrons pass through an external circuit creating useful energy at around 0.7 volts then recombining with protons at the cathode to produce water (see Fig. 7.2).

To build up a useful voltage, cells are stacked between conductive bipolar plates, usually graphite, which have integral channels to allow the free flow of hydrogen and oxygen (see Fig. 7.3).

The electrical efficiency of the PEMFC is 35% with a target of 45%. Its energy density is 0.3 kW/kg compared with 1.0 kW/kg for internal combustion engines.

One problem with the PEMFC is that it requires hydrogen of a high degree of purity. Research activity is focusing on finding cheaper and more robust catalysts as well as more efficient ion exchange polymer electrolytes.

Originally the PEMFCs were conceived for vehicle application. Now they are being developed to supply single homes or housing estates with electricity and heat. Approximately the same amount of heat and electricity are generated. Initially the hydrogen fuel will be obtained from reformed natural gas supplied through existing networks. Rather optimistically the journal *New Scientist* in its editorial (25 November 2000) predicted that 'Within a couple of years, fuel cells will provide heat and power for homes and offices'. It goes on to suggest that cheap gas will enable fuel cells 'to undercut today's combination of

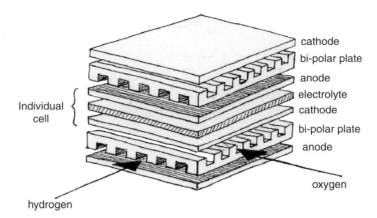

cathode
bi-polar plate
anode
electrolyte
cathode
bi-polar plate
anode

Individual cell

oxygen

hydrogen

Figure 7.3 Fuel cell stack

heating boiler and mains electricity'. It is more likely that 2008 will be the date by which fuel cell combined heat and power will start to penetrate the domestic market.

However, it has already penetrated the sphere of transport. Buses in the city of Vancouver have been operating Ballard PEMFCs since 1993. The cells deliver 125 h.p. and the buses have a range of 100 miles. The Chicago Transit Authority hopes to substitute this technology for all its 2000 buses. London has a fleet of six fuel cell buses as a demonstration project.

California was the pioneer in placing restrictions on fossil fuel vehicles. It planned that 10% of cars in the state would be powered by hydrogen by 2004 but it had to capitulate to the massed ranks of the automotive lobby.

Italy has an accelerating problem of pollution from vehicles. The Lombardy region is particularly affected with its capital Milan experiencing smog levels five times the legal limit. The result is that the regional government was considering a ban on the sales of all petrol and diesel cars after 2005. It is unlikely that there will, in the near to medium-term future, be a network access to pure hydrogen for vehicles. In the interim it is most likely the gas will be catalysed from methanol.

Phosphoric acid fuel cell (PAFC)

Similar to PEMFCs, this cell operates in the middle temperature range at around 200°C. This means it can tolerate some impurities. It employs a phosphoric acid proton conducting electrolyte and platinum or platinum–rhodium electrodes. The main difference from a PEMFC is that it uses a liquid electrolyte.

The system efficiency is currently in the 37–43% range, but this is expected to improve. This technology seems particularly popular in Japan where electricity costs are high and dispersed generation is preferred. A 200 kW unit which uses sewage gas provides heat and power for Yokohama sewage works. The largest installation to date for the Tokyo Electric Power Company had an output of 11 megawatts until it finally expired.

PAFC units have been used experimentally in buses. However, it is likely that its future lies in stationary systems.

The *New Scientist* editorial referred to above predicts that 'Larger, static fuel cells will become attractive for hotels and sports centres, while power companies will use them as alternatives to extending the electricity grid'. An example of this is the police station in

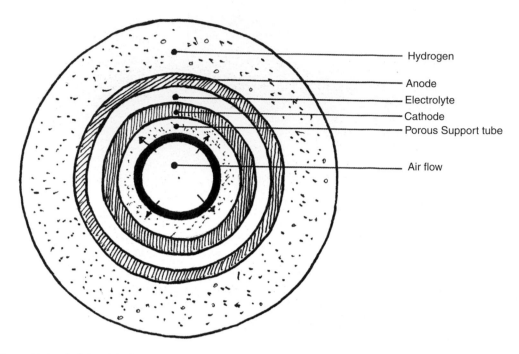

Hydrogen

Anode
Electrolyte
Cathode
Porous Support tube

Air flow

Figure 7.4   Solid oxide fuel cell (SOFC) in its tubular configuration

Central Park, New York, which found that installing a PAFC of 200 kW capacity was cheaper than a grid connection requiring new cables in the park. One year after this prediction the Borough of Woking, Surrey, UK installed the first commercial PAFC fuel cell to operate in the UK. It also has a capacity of 200 kW and is providing heat, cooling, light and dehumidification for the Pool in the Park recreation centre. The fuel cell forms part of Working Park's larger combined heat and power system.

Solid oxide fuel cell (SOFCs)

This is a cell suitable only for static application, taking several hours to reach its operating temperature. It is a high-temperature cell, running at between 800 and 1000°C. Its great virtue is that it can run on a range of fuels including natural gas and methanol which can be reformed within the cell. Its high operating temperature also enables it to break down impurities. Its high temperature also removes the need for noble metal catalysts such as platinum.

It potentially has a wide range of power outputs, from 1 to 1000 kW.

In contrast to PEMFCs the electrolyte conducts oxygen ions rather than hydrogen ions which move from the cathode to the anode. The electrolyte is a ceramic which becomes conductive to oxygen ions at 800°C. SOFCs are often structured in a tubular rather than a planar form (as in the PEMFC) to reduce the chance of failure of the seals due to high-temperature expansion. Air (oxygen) flows through a central tube whilst fuel flows round the outside of the structure (see Fig. 7.4).

According to David Hart,

> *Solid oxide fuel cells are expected to have the widest range of applications. Large units should be useful in industry for generating electricity and heat. Smaller units could be used in houses.*[3]

Figure 7.5   Micro-fuel cell by Ceres Power (courtesy of Ceres Power, www.cerespower.com)

As confirmation of his prophecy, Ceres Power has developed a 1 kW SOFC designed for the domestic market, producing heat and power (Fig. 7.5). It is fuelled by natural gas which British Gas claims will make it accessible to 14.5 million households. It should be market-ready in 2007.

There is confidence that the installed cost of static high-temperature fuel cells will fall to $600–1000 per kW. As cogeneration power units this will make them highly competitive with conventional systems. Already SOFCs are now being imported to the UK from the USA at a cost of $1000 per kilowatt, which brings them closer to cost-effectiveness in comparison to fossil fuels which continue to rise in cost.

One of the main producers of SOFCs is Westinghouse, USA, which uses the tubular configuration for the cell.

A 200 kW unit has been installed on a test basis in The Netherlands.

Alkaline fuel cells (AFCs)

This fuel cell dates back to the 1940s and was the first to be fully developed in the 1960s. It was used in the Apollo spacecraft programme. It employs an alkaline electrolyte such as potassium hydroxide set between nickel or precious metal electrodes. Its operating temperature is 60–80°C which enables it to have a short warm-up time.

Its main drawback is that the electrolyte reacts with carbon dioxide which significantly reduces its performance. This means it has to use pure hydrogen and oxygen as its fuels. Another problem is that it has an energy density one tenth that of PEMFCs, which makes it much bulkier for a given output. On the plus side it is relatively cheap and has a role in static applications.

Molten carbonate fuel cells (MCFCs)

This is a high-temperature fuel cell operating at about 650°C. The electrolyte in this case is an alkaline mixture of lithium and potassium carbonates which becomes liquid at 650°C and is supported by a ceramic matrix. The electrodes are both nickel-based. The operation of the MCFC differs from that of other fuel cells in that it involves carbonate ion transfer across the electrolyte. This makes it tolerate both carbon monoxide and carbon dioxide. The cell can consume hydrocarbon fuels that are reformed into hydrogen within the cell.

The MCFC can achieve an efficiency of 55%. The steam and carbon dioxide it produces can be used to drive a turbine generator (cogeneration) which can raise the total efficiency to 80% – up to twice that of a typical oil- or gas-fired plant. Consequently this technology could be ideal for urban power stations producing combined heat and power. The Energy Research Corporation (ERC) of Danbury, Connecticut, USA has built a two-megawatt unit for the municipality of Santa Clara, California, and that company is currently developing a 2.85 megawatt plant.

Development programmes in Japan and the USA have produced small prototype units in the 5–20 kW range, which, if successful, will make them attractive for domestic combined heat and power.

The main disadvantage of the MCFC is that it uses as electrolytes highly corrosive molten salts that create both design and maintenance problems.

Research is concentrating on solutions to these problems.

In March 2000 it was announced that researchers in the University of Pennsylvania in Philadelphia had developed a cell that could run directly off natural gas or methane. It did not have to be reformed to produce hydrogen. Most other fuel cells cannot run directly on hydrocarbons which clog the catalyst within minutes.

At the RIBA conference of October 2001 which triggered this book, Professor Tony Marmont offered a scenario whereby the fuel cell in a car would operate in conjunction with a home or office. He estimated that a car spends 96% of its time stationary so it would make sense to couple the car to a building to provide space and domestic hot water heat. The electricity generated, amounting to about 50–80 kW, would be sold to the grid. The car would be fuelled by a hydrogen grid. Until that is available a catalyser within the car would reform methanol to provide the hydrogen. However, if the natural gas cell proves its worth, then it would simply draw its energy from the domestic supply.

Considerable research activity is focusing on fuel cells, particularly on how to reduce the costs of catalysts and improve energy density. One promising research programme is investigating how an enzyme substitute can break hydrogen molecules into their constituent atoms. The goal is a cheap catalyst which could transform the cost-effectiveness of fuel cells. The principle is to mimic the hydrogenase enzyme, adding ruthenium, which performs most of the hydrogen-splitting operation. Ruthenium is up to fifteen times cheaper than the conventional platinum.

Hydrogen, the agent of social reform

At present consumers of energy in developed countries are reliant on either an extensive grid of wires or pipes for gas. Both are wasteful of energy and costly in terms of maintenance (Fig. 7.6).

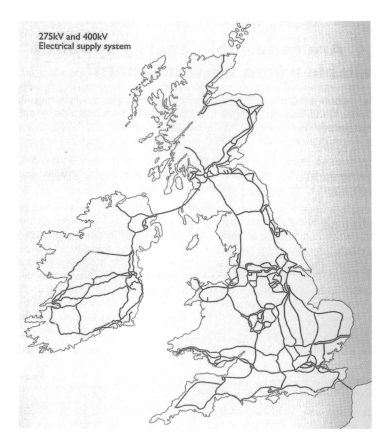

275kV and 400kV
Electrical supply system

Figure 7.6   The National Grid for the UK and Ireland including the inter-connectors with Ireland and the continent

One of the most persuasive of hydrogen apologists is Jeremy Rifkin, particularly in his latest book *The Hydrogen Economy: The Creation of the Worldwide Energy Web.*

According to him, the true destiny of fuel cells is fundamentally to change the relationship between people and energy which he calls 'The Next Great Economic and Social Revolution'.

Fuel cells suitable for commercial or domestic application are now available which opens up the possibility of an entirely new architecture for access to energy, namely distributed generation. It is the beginning of the transformation from a top-down energy supply system to one that is localized or 'bottom-up'. Individual companies or householders will be producers as well as consumers of energy. As Rifkin puts it. 'When millions of end-users connect their fuel cells powered by renewables into local, regional and national publicly owned hydrogen energy webs (HEWs), they can begin to share energy peer-to-peer – creating a new decentralized form of energy generation and use'.

Rifkin is convinced that the decentralized energy web will have a combined generating power in excess of that provided by the power utility companies. Advanced computers will transform the grid into a 'fully interactive intelligent energy network. Sensors and intelligent agents embedded throughout the system can provide up-to-the moment information on energy conditions, allowing current to flow exactly where and when it is needed and at the cheapest price'.[4]

Many have pointed out that the lack of energy is a key factor in maintaining world poverty. As the cost of fuel cells and electrolysing equipment continues to fall through technology improvements and economies of scale, PV/wind/biomass etc. generated electricity will enable remote villages to have their own mini-grid, with continuity of supply ensured by a community fuel cell, probably of the solid oxide variety. It may be more cost-effective for the fuel cell to be leased. As Rifkin puts it: 'Co-operatives, lending institutions and local governments might then view distributed generation energy webs as a core strategy for building sustainable, self-sufficient communities. Breaking the cycle of dependency and despair, becoming truly "empowered", starts with access to, and control over, energy'.[5]

For a variety of technical reasons the widespread adoption of fuel cell technology is some way off. Of course, if the hydrogen were to be carbon-free during production as well as use and the avoided external costs were to be translated into a subsidy, then hydrogen would already be cost-effective.

Several factors are already coalescing to make the fuel cell vehicle more attractive to the market than its fossil fuel powered counterpart:

- the inexorable rise in oil and gas prices
- rising uncertainty over secure supplies through a combination of resource depletion and an increasingly destabilized Middle East
- present generation internal combustion engine vehicles are nearing the peak of their efficiency which the industry regards as 30%. With the international research being directed towards fuel cell technology, it is very possible that their efficiency will rise from 50% now to at least 60%
- with increasing world population and an expanding middle class in the developing world, it is predicted that demand for cars will grow exponentially adding to the need to develop alternatives to fossil fuels.

Fuel cells and the UK

In December 2004 a research project funded by the DTI and led by Eoin Lees, former Chief Executive of the Energy Saving Trust, examined the prospects for hydrogen in the UK.[6]

Its final report came to the following conclusions:

'The UK's priorities with regard to hydrogen were unclear making them hard to address for the purpose of achieving maximum overall benefit. Hydrogen energy support was provided by several initiatives in the UK but a dedicated programme was not in place. . . The UK had no clear means to engage in international initiatives'.

This is a fair summary of the UK's current position.

In 2004 the Tyndall Centre at the University of East Angila summarized stakeholder attitudes to fuel cells, especially identifying barriers to progress with the technology.

The key conclusion of the research was that 'insufficient governmental support has been given to enable fuel cells to develop properly as a credible alternative energy technology'.[7]

This refers not only to regulatory matters like the New Electricity Trading Arrangement (NETA) which particularly penalizes renewables and small generators, but also the paucity of financial support through subsidy or tax concessions. Stakeholders identified the high costs of development of the technology as a main barrier to bringing it to commercial viability. It is the familiar story that fuel cells do not offer adequate short term returns when valued against conventional fossil-based energy. Government support for demonstration projects in both static and mobile applications is vital if fuel cells are to become marketable.

Another problem was that fuel cells are still considered to be an innovative and untried technology that have still to prove their worth as an alternative power source. Added to this is the inertia within the energy industry due mainly to the vested interests of the main fossil-fuel-based generators.

Within the renewable energy community there is debate as to whether fuel cells are appropriate if it takes electricity via water electrolysis to produce hydrogen to power a fuel cell which produces electricity. Would it not be better to use direct electricity from PVs, wind, etc., for static applications? The virtue of the fuel cell is that it guarantees continuity of supply. Increasingly sophisticated electronic devices are highly sensitive to micro-second disruptions of supply (power outages) and where this is a factor fuel cells can already be cost-effective.

There is also the problem that, at the present rate of installation, it will be a considerable time before renewables generate enough surplus power to create reserves of hydrogen that will ensure that the fuel cell is a carbon free technology.

It was recognized by stakeholders that, in the long term, fuel cells will be the major power source for transport. In the medium term it was considered that static cells would predominate, especially if the Government's alleged support for distributed generation results in legislative and financial support for this alternative infrastructure. A strategy paper of 2004 from the regulator Ofgem called 'Distributed generation – the way forward' gives weight to this argument. It sets out the ways in which small scale renewables can be integrated into the distribution network. Others are convinced that transport will lead the way.

The three main conclusions of the research were:

- Stationary fuel cells offer 'a significant way forward towards sustainable energy'. But, there are still problems associated with the carbon emissions involved in the production of hydrogen. There are also concerns about the costs involved in creating a hydrogen infrastructure.
- The UK Government has not given adequate support to the development of fuel cell technology including storage systems. Most participants in the research considered that the Government was not convinced about the inevitability of the hydrogen economy in general and fuel cells in particular.
- Thirdly, the lack of demonstration models in the UK is undermining the development of the technology. More demonstrations at varying scales of output, supported by Government subsidy, would demonstrate its commitment to what most nations consider to be the future for energy. Financial support for the integration of fuel cell CHP into new housing would provide an ideal demonstration opportunity, especially if integrated with other forms of renewable energy.

Perhaps the greatest beneficiaries of the transition to a hydrogen-based energy infrastructure will be rural communities in developing countries who could never hope to be connected to a grid supply. Access to energy is the main factor which divides the rich from the poor throughout the world. A cheap fuel cell powered by hydrogen electrolysed from PV, solar-electric or small-scale hydroelectricity could be the ultimate answer to this unacceptable inequality.

There is little doubt that we are approaching the threshold of the hydrogen-based economy. Ultimately hydrogen should be available 'on tap' through a piped network. In the meantime reforming natural gas, petrol, propane and other hydrocarbons to produce hydrogen would still result in massive reductions in carbon dioxide emissions and pollutants like oxides of sulphur and nitrogen. The domestic scale fuel cells about to be marketed will have built-in processing units to reform hydrocarbon fuels and the whole system will occupy about the same space as a central heating boiler.

One of the stumbling blocks to the widespread adoption of fuel cells is the fact that hydrogen has to be 'liberated' from water or hydrocarbon fuels. In the case of water the process employs an electrolyser which is effectively a fuel cell in reverse. Standard electrolysers use platinum as the catalyst on both the hydrogen and oxygen electrodes to split water into its constituents of hydrogen and oxygen. Significant advances in the chemistry of electrolysers has been claimed by ITM Power plc, which has substituted nickel as the hydrogen electrode. This significantly reduces the cost. These economies will also apply to fuel cells.[8]

Nuclear fusion

For many decades nuclear fusion has been the pot of gold at the end of the energy rainbow. For most of the time it has been the province of high-energy physics. One favourite strategy has been to fuse two deuterium atoms: hydrogen with a neutron. The fusion of the two creates a massive surge of energy. The reaction can create hydrogen and radioactive tritium. The latter has a half-life of 12 years and can be turned into helium by fusing it with more deuterium. Compared with nuclear fission, it is a clean technology, producing minimal amounts of waste.

The stumbling block is that, in order to overcome the repulsive forces between the nuclei within the deuterium, the deuterium has to be heated to 10,000°C, the temperature at the heart of the sun. Maintaining the stability of matter at such a temperature is extremely difficult and consumes massive amounts of energy. As yet it has proved impossible to generate more energy from the process than is required to create the reaction. The theoretical belief is that ultimately fusion will create a net surplus of energy by a factor of ten. As the international energy scene becomes increasingly volatile, a huge research effort into fusion is focused on a massive facility in Japan. It is slowly graduating from the possible to the probable.

Notes

1. *New Scientist*, 'Inside Science, Fuelling the Future' 16 June 2001
2. US National Renewable Energy Laboratory (NREL)
3. David Hart, op cit, p. 3
4. *emagazine.com*, 'After oil, clean energy from a fuel-cell-driven global hydrogen web' December 2005, p.5
5. *emagazine.com*, op cit, p.8
6. Energy Saving Trust, 'A strategic framework for hydrogen energy in the UK' December 2004
7. Peters, M. D. and Powell, J. C., Working Paper 64, November 2004
8. www.itm-power.com

8 Bioenergy

Biomass is the sum total of all the Earth's living matter within the biosphere. It is continually regenerated by the sun through the process of photosynthesis. The energy reaching the planet is equivalent to about seven times its primary energy consumption. If biomass is converted to a fuel when it is at its peak as a store of chemical energy the process is carbon neutral. This means that the carbon emitted when it is burnt is equal to the carbon absorbed during growth. It is not a complete zero sum since there is a carbon component in the energy used in accumulating, processing and transporting the biomass.

Biomass conversion falls into two categories:

- cultivated short rotation crops
- biomass from waste.

Biomass produces energy from a variety of sources:

- fast-growing trees and shrubs, for example, willow, poplar, miscanthus
- residues from agricultural crops and forest thinning and felling
- animal waste, liquid and solid, such as poultry litter
- industrial residues, for example from saw mills
- municipal solid waste.

Biofuels fall into two categories:

- *dedicated* sources such as short rotation crops, e.g. coppiced willow
- *dependent* sources, which are the remains of a primary crop such as wheat and maize – the stubble or wheat straw and the stems and stocks of corn remaining after the crop has been harvested are significant sources of bioenergy.

There are three main systems for converting biomass to energy:

- direct combustion
- anaerobic digestion from organic waste producing biogas
- landfill gas conversion.

Utilization of biofuels

Direct combustion

Short-rotation coppice (SRC) of certain fast-growing trees like willow can provide a bulk fuel for burning in power plants. It can be co-fired with coal to reduce emissions and prolong the life of coal-fired plants. Trees are planted at a rate of 15,000 per hectare and cut back to near ground level after a year. They usually re-grow as multiple stems and after two to four years can be harvested for fuel. The cycle is repeated over a life span of about 30 years.

One problem in a liberalized energy market is the compatibility between an agricultural process and an industrial process of producing electricity. Power producers have to guarantee power in 30-minute intervals at an agreed price and predicted four hours in advance. Failure to meet this challenge resulted in the demise of the ARBRE project in Yorkshire.

In the first edition of this book there was a section devoted to the ARBRE project (Arable Biomass Renewable Energy project), the UK's first biomass to biogas enterprise. It was designed to process short-rotation coppice willow and produce 10 MW of electricity. Early in 2003 the project was put into the hands of the receivers and 50 farmers, who had been encouraged to grow the necessary crops, were left without a market. This included a farm near Retford in Nottinghamshire owned by John Strawson, which had dedicated 11% of the farmland amounting to 172 ha to the crop. The two alternatives were either to abandon SRC altogether or find an alternative use for the crops. In opting for the second route most of the farmers agreed to revert to producing feedstock for thermal power stations and smaller market opportunities. A company called Renewable Energy Growers Ltd was formed in 2004 with 45 of the original growers. Renewable Energy Suppliers was formed shortly afterwards by John Strawson of Manor. He invented a novel mechanical process to reduce willow to the fine and consistent gauge of 3 to 10 mm that would enable it to be mixed with coal in a conventional power station. Granule sizes up 30 mm are also produced for a variety of installations as well as billets for domestic stoves and fires (see Fig. 8.1).

The energy density of the fuel is 15 gigajoules per tonne at a moisture content of 20–25%.

The willow is harvested in a three-year cycle and the 172 ha of willow yields 1720 oven-dried tonnes (ODT) per year to the coal-fired power station of Drax in Yorkshire and Cottam in Nottinghamshire under contract. Unfortunately, Drax recently declined to renew the contract. Altogether the Renewable Energy Supplies produced 3500 tonnes of willow in various forms including 'granules' in 2005–6. This is equivalent to a saving in carbon dioxide of 6125 tonnes. Renewable Energy Suppliers market their high-quality product as 'Koolfuel', which amounts to 75% of the total energy crop delivered to the energy markets in the UK.

Unlike most renewable energy sources, the economics of SRC willow compare favourably with conventional fuels. With recent price increases for fossil fuels it is likely that this is now the cheapest fuel. In the domestic sector even in 2003 it was the cheapest fuel.

Is this fuel truly carbon neutral? The standard equation is that the CO_2 taken up in growth is returned to the atmosphere when burnt. However, some of the growth carbon is retained in the roots. On the other hand there is the carbon involved in the processing and transportation etc. The safest claim is that it is as near carbon neutral as any other form of renewable energy.

To maximize the opportunities presented by the SRC willow operation, Strawsons have developed a business park within the farm complex. After only one full year in operation the enterprise was now providing fuel for a number of enterprises with biomass heat boilers including business parks, schools, district and local heating installations and domestic developments.

Figure 8.1   Processing and cutting of willow, Manor Farm (courtesy of Renewable Energy Suppliers Ltd)

This is a qualified success story thanks to the persistence of the people involved in overcoming the many obstacles that are encountered whenever novel enterprises seek to break the mould.

The UK government is currently supporting a project to grow elephant grass – a giant tropical plant reaching up to 3.5 m – ultimately over 180,000 ha. A power station to burn this type of crop is nearing completion in Eccleshall, Staffordshire. Drax is also earmarked to use this crop and farmland around Drax will supply it. The question arises as to whether this constitutes a direct threat to SRC willow since there is possibly a limit to which a large coal-fired plant like Drax can accommodate biofuels.

Energy from wood waste

At the moment the majority of waste from forest maintenance, furniture manufacture and other timber-related activities is not exploited for energy. At Renewable Energy Suppliers it is utilized, creating wood pellets in a compact and easy-to-use form of biomass fuel suitable for domestic and district heating. This is a near carbon neutral source of energy produced by compressing wood waste under high pressure into cylinders or billets about 10 cm in diameter and 10–30 cm long. They have a low moisture content, giving them a high energy density.

Such manufacturing plants range from 100 tonnes to 10,000 tonnes a year capacity. Billets are produced from a variety of feedstocks but the most effective are shavings and sawdust. However, other feedstocks like tree bark straw and other crop residues can be used, though they are more suitable for industrial scale plants than domestic use. There is a growing market in domestic pellet stoves and boilers, especially in Germany and Austria. An Austrian 12 kW central heating pellet boiler is designed to operate in conjunction with solar thermal heating. In Scandinavia, pellets are widely used for district heating. In Denmark there is a power station that uses 300,000 wood pellets a year to produce 570 MWe (electricity) and 570 MWth (heat) a year. Such plants commonly derive 50% of their energy from pellets to achieve up to 95% efficiency. As the price of oil crosses the $70 a barrel threshold so wood pellets become increasingly cost-effective – even in the UK.

Work began early in 2006 on a £90 million biomass heat and power plant by the power company E.oN at Steven's Croft near Lockerbie, Scotland. It will burn 220,000 tonnes per year of forest waste, producing enough power for about 70,000 homes. In this connection the Deputy First Minister for Scotland affirmed that his country 'has abundant resources to lead the way in biomass development in the UK, providing and sustaining jobs and meeting local energy needs . . . . we can help make Scotland a powerhouse for renewable energy'.

A perennial problem facing renewable energy in all its forms is the planning regime. In one instance a farmer in Cornwall converted to producing rapid rotation crops for a thermal plant that was due to be built nearby. For crops to be available requires several years of lead-in time. In the event, the plant was refused planning permission, which highlights a problem that bedevils the whole renewables spectrum.

On the positive side a 36 MW straw burning plant, the Elan Power Station in Cambridgeshire, is the largest in the world and 'a noted success'.[1] Equally successful are three thermal energy plants in the UK, burning mostly poultry litter with a total capacity of 64.7 MW.

Poultry litter, which is a mixture of chicken manure and straw or wood shavings, is a viable form of fuel for electricity generation in rural areas. The largest plant in the UK is a 39 MW installation in Scotland.

Bioenergy is a reliable source of power and, as such, can act as back-up or 'spinning reserve' for intermittent renewables. 'Improved financial and political support from governments is, however, of great importance to the commercial success of the whole biomass industry both in terms of generating investor confidence and ensuring that plants are economically viable on start-up'.[2]

Municipal solid waste

The increasing cost of landfill disposal of household waste and the growing scarcity of sites is encouraging the incineration of municipal solid waste (MSW) which is increasingly being used to generate both heat and power on a municipal scale. Examples include Sheffield Heat and Power, which generates electricity for the grid whilst providing low-grade heat for the city centre, the universities and hospitals. Another example is the South East London Combined Heat and Power (CHP) Plant designed to burn 420,000 tonnes of MSW a year, producing steam for a 31 MW turbo-generator.

There have been concerns about emissions from incinerators such as heavy metals and organic compounds such as dioxins. However, the EU is imposing increasingly stringent emissions standards. Currently energy from waste accounts for 0.1% of all UK dioxin emissions.

The burning of biomass to generate steam to drive turbines for combined heat and power is the most common method of deriving energy either from waste or energy crops. However, gasification is the preferred method for large-scale systems of >10 MW. Conversion of coal-fired plants which can co-fire biomass is a medium-term economic option.

Anaerobic digestion from waste

Anaerobic digestion (AD) is becoming increasingly important as a means of disposing of waste. Germany, with 1500 small farm-based digestion plants, and Denmark, with its centralized plants producing combined heat and power, are among the leaders.

In this process, wet waste comprising dung or sewage is transformed into a slurry with about 95% water content. This mixture is fed to a sealed digester where the temperature can be controlled. Digesters range in size from a domestic scale holding ~200 gallons to up to 1000 m^3 for industrial-size installations. The digestion process involves the breaking down by bacteria of organic material into sugars and then into various acids. These

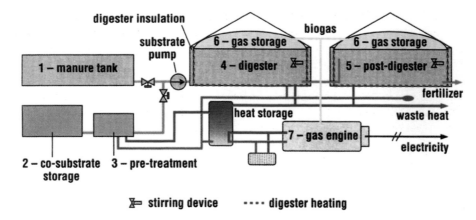

Figure 8.2 Diagram of a farm scale anaerobic digestion plant (courtesy of *Renewable Energy World* March/April 2004)

decompose to produce the final gas. The action of the bacteria generates heat and, in temperate climes, this usually has to be augmented to maintain a temperature of between 35 and 60°C. The heat can be provided by utilizing some of the biogas produced by the process.

The biogas consists of about 65% methane (CH_4) and 35% CO_2. Biogas can be used to provide heat and electricity. It can power conventional combustion engines to provide electricity and contribute to the heat required for digestion. If it is treated to remove hydrogen sulphide and CO_2 it is virtually the same as natural gas and can be used to power vehicles. Most spark ignition engines can be modified to run on this fuel.

In total the energy content of waste from farm animals in the UK is around 100 PJ. However, the accessible energy is in the region of 10 PJ which relates to an installed capacity of ~100 MW (see Fig. 8.2).

Biogas can be processed to serve the piped network. To use natural gas pipelines it has to be processed as follows:

- large scale removal of CO_2 to 3–6%
- removal of fine particles and other trace components
- drying
- desulphurization
- odorization.

The processing of municipal sewage and farm waste offers the greatest long-term potential for biogas. However, the main deterrent to widespread use is cost. In the current costings the environmental gains are not factored in. 'With legislation in place to protect the environment, biogas plants would be far more economic . . . . government support mechanisms are currently required to make biogas plants commercially attractive.'[3]

The technology has been proven for a considerable time but it suffers from the cost-effectiveness anomaly yardstick set by subsidised co-generation gas-fired plants.

Landfill methane

The focus in the UK for anaerobic digestion has been on landfill methane, which can be extracted at much less cost since the digestion process takes place naturally underground. However, on the European scale, this source is expected to diminish rapidly after 2006.[4] The UK should not be much different.

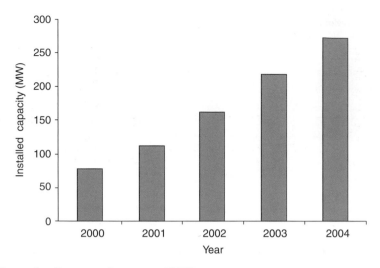

Figure 8.3   Biogas for Germany (courtesy *REW*)

Examples

At Laholm, Sweden, a community biogas plant was installed in 1992 to process 25,000 tonnes of liquid manure per year and 10,000 tonnes of other waste. In 2001 a processing plant was set up to raise biogas to natural gas quality. In 2003 the plant provided 30% of the gas distributed in Laholm. At Linkoping the municipal bus fleet of 63 vehicles and 132 other vehicles is powered by biogas. The biogas production plant operates simultaneously as a waste treatment facility producing vehicle fuel and a manufacturer of fertilizers.

At the present time Germany and Austria offer the best investment opportunities for anaerobic digestion, the reason being the relatively high feed-in tariffs: 15 Eurocents/kWh guaranteed for 15 years for Germany and 14.5 Eurocents for 13 years for Austria. The effect can be judged by the development of the technology in Germany since 1999 (see Fig. 8.3).

The UK by comparison produces almost as much manure as Germany but only a small fraction is converted to energy. It is still a long way from realizing its potential which, according to the Royal Commission on Environmental Pollution, is 16 GW of energy[5] (generating capacity is measured in watts).

This is particularly the case in terms of anaerobic digestion energy (Fig. 8.4).

Output over a given period or delivered energy is measured in joules (see p. 15).

Output is also measured in millions of tonnes of oil equivalent (mtoe) and kilowatt hours (kWh).

In the UK about 70% of all sewage is now treated by means of anaerobic digestion. By 1994 33 MW of electricity was produced under the Non-Fossil Fuel Obligation (NFFO). Following the abolition of the NFFO there have been very few new projects. However, many plants use the biogas to provide heat and electricity for site use.

One of the key problems for the UK is that there is no government biofuel strategy. 'There is considerable policy inertia because existing UK policy governs such large amounts of primary energy, some 225 mtoe [2002], of which roughly 90% is fossil fuel based. Such a lop-sided fuel mix makes it difficult for new primary fuels to make inroads.'[6]

Note: in 2005 fossil fuels accounted for 72% of the energy mix.

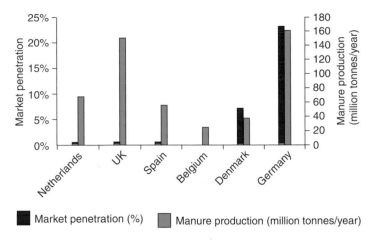

Figure 8.4 Market penetration of anaerobic digestion compared with manure production in the reviewed European countries (courtesy of *REW*)

Biofuel for transport

Biofuel for transport is a further opportunity sector for biomass. Revisions to the EU Common Agricultural Policy which came into effect in 2005 pose a challenge to farmers as world cereal prices fall. Energy crops are an obvious substitute. The Department of Environment, Food and Rural Affairs (Defra) is currently investigating barriers to energy crop production. Already the EU is the largest producer of biodiesel in the world at 500,000 tonnes with the potential for twice that capacity. Italy, France, Germany, Belgium and Austria are the main producers.

For many decades Brazil has been the world leader in the use of bioethanol derived from sugar. Half its new cars are tuned to run on 100% ethanol. Sweden is setting the pace in Europe. Saab has introduced a model which runs on 85% ethanol and two thirds of advance orders are for this model. Volvo is following the Saab example. If this is deemed to be innovative technology it must be remembered that Henry Ford recommended ethanol in favour of gasoline, fearing the southern states might deprive the north of oil.

Rapeseed yields ~3.2 t/ha with 37% recoverable oil with 95% conversion to diesel giving 0.4 million tonnes of oil per year or 0.5% of UK oil demand. Conversion to diesel needs the addition of methanol from biological sources.

In June 2005 The Worldwatch Institute of Washington teamed up with the German Ministry for Consumer Protection and Agriculture to investigate the global potential for the large-scale use of biofuels for transportation. This has been prompted by growing concerns over the security of supply of oil combined with the relentless rise in its price. Over the previous three years the market for biofuels grew by 70% suggesting that this was the time to 'assess strategies for maximizing the economic, social and environmental benefits of biofuels development'.[7] The project is being funded by the German government.

Due to be completed in July 2006, the project will seek to quantify the potential for biofuels to displace petroleum fuels and will assess the policy instruments in place to stimulate their production. Included in the project will be an assessment of 'the broader impacts of large-scale development of biofuels, focusing on the implications for the size of farms, the health of rural communities, the energy and chemical requirements of agriculture, impacts on rural landscapes and biodiversity, air and water quality, climate change and international trade balances'.[8]

The purpose of the project is to collaborate with the German government to devise 'cutting-edge policies for the development of a vibrant biofuels industry'.

Introducing a debate on Renewable Energy in the House of Lords on 23 June 2005, Lord Oxburgh described how a small enzyme company, Iogen, had developed an enzyme that can break down straw into its constituent sugars to produce cellulose ethanol. In collaboration with Shell (of which Lord Oxburgh was Chairman to June 2005) it is making an ethanol fuel from what had previously been a waste product. The process involves fermentation and distillation to produce Ecoethanol, so named to distinguish it from ethanol derived from corn and wheat. In the latter case only a small fraction of the plant is used for fuel and the rest wasted. It is expected that, when it is in full production, it will be significantly cheaper than fuel oil. For a brief period in May 2005 even corn ethanol was cheaper in the US than gasoline.

The advantages of cellulose ethanol are:

- its processing does not involve fossil fuels; instead it uses plant by-products to create the energy to run the process
- the effect is a net zero greenhouse gas product
- the raw material, being a waste product, does not compete as a human food source and exploits existing farm practices
- the agricultural industry produces large quantities of residue which is mostly burned or left to enrich the soil; however, the practice of burning is becoming increasingly unpopular and, in some countries, illegal. There is huge scope for converting this residue into cellulose ethanol
- until recently, expensive and inefficient bioprocesses made cellulose ethanol uneconomic, but developments in biotechnology and process technology have made large-scale cellulose ethanol production a reality which promises to revolutionize the transport industry.

A UK Biomass Task Force reported in June 2005 on the outlook for biofuels and concluded that 500,000 ha could be devoted to growing oil seed crops with a similar area dedicated to wheat and root crops for bioethanol. In 2002 the Institute of Biology (IoB) concluded that this area planted with Miscanthus could produce 3 million tonnes of oil equivalent of biofuel, representing 4% of annual oil demand. In total the IoB reckons that biofuels could offset UK primary energy demand by 7%, the equivalent of 16 million tonnes of domestic oil consumption.

The government has stated its intention to introduce a Renewable Transport Fuels Obligation by April 2008, which will require diesel and petrol to be blended with 5% biodiesel or bioethanol.

Summary

Biomass is the sum total of the Earth's living matter. It is potentially near carbon neutral if used as a solid, liquid or gaseous fuel. Conversion of biomass to be suitable as a fuel falls into two categories:

- from waste
- by cultivation of short rotation crops.

There are three main methods of conversion to energy:

- direct combustion
- anaerobic digestion
- extraction of landfill methane.

In direct combustion SRCs provide bulk for burning directly in power plants or co-fired with coal. In anaerobic digestion, wet waste including sewage is fed into a sealed digester. Bacteria break down the biomass to produce a methane-rich gas which can be used to generate combined heat and power. Suitably treated biogas can be introduced into the natural gas pipe network.

Landfill methane is the most abundant source of biogas but reserves are expected to decline rapidly.

Considerable opportunities exist for biofuels to power transport. Brazil has been doing it for decades. A research project funded by Germany is considering the potential of biodiesel and bioethanol to replace petrol products with the aim of producing a 'vibrant biofuels industry'.

One of the most promising routes for the future is a project that involves an enzyme that breaks down straw into its constituent sugars to produce cellulose ethanol. Further distillation produces a product marketed as Ecoethanol.

The 2005 Biomass Task Force anticipates that 1 million ha will be available for biofuels.

Notes

1. *REW* January/February 2005
2. 'Global growth: The world biomass market', Bruce Knight and Alan Westwood, *REW*, January/February 2005, pp. 118–127
3. Ian French, author of the Frost and Sullivan report on the European biogas sector. *REW* July/August 2003, pp. 120–131
4. *REW* January/February 2005, p. 127
5. Royal Commission on Environmental Pollution report, May 2004
6. 'Fuelling the Future 3 – Biofuels', report by the Institute of Biology and British Crop Protection Council, February 2002
7. Worldwatch Web News June 27 2005

9 Microgeneration and combined heat and power

In March 2006 the UK government issued a report outlining a new microgeneration programme called 'Our energy strategy power from the people'. It was prompted by the Energy Saving Trust's (EST) prediction that microgeneration could provided 30–40% of the UK's electricity needs by 2050. The report was mainly descriptive, identifying a range of difficulties faced by potential installers, particularly the problems of contributing to the grid and the feed-in tariffs that are offered. Its main conclusion was there needs to be a clear idea of the real potential of all microgeneration technologies before setting a target. Setting targets is justified if there are to be subsidies to encourage the adoption of these technologies. Otherwise it is all up to the vagaries of the market and targets are mere wishful thinking.

Much of the research has already been done by the EST with a study which shows the current status of these technologies and their expected break-even dates (see Fig. 9.1).

It is worth noting that only the micro-solid oxide fuel cell and Stirling combined heat and power technologies ultimately break even without any subsidy.

Micropower and CHP

There is an increasing climate of opinion in favour of 'distributed' or decentralized power generation. This is especially the case in rural locations or where stability of supply is essential, such as for banks, hospitals research facilities etc. Micropower or small-scale generation is the key to this trend.

There are several advantages to this alternative to the large-scale grid system served by a few large thermal power plants:

- Small-scale power can be closer to the point of use, overcoming the inefficiency of long distribution lines.
- It can be scaled to meet the exact requirements of the consumer. For example, in the USA domestic consumers use an average rate of 1.5 kW.
- In most of its versions it has a relatively high efficiency by producing both electricity and heat.
- There are considerable environmental cost avoidance benefits.
- In some cases it is modular, meaning that it can be scaled up or down to meet changing needs.

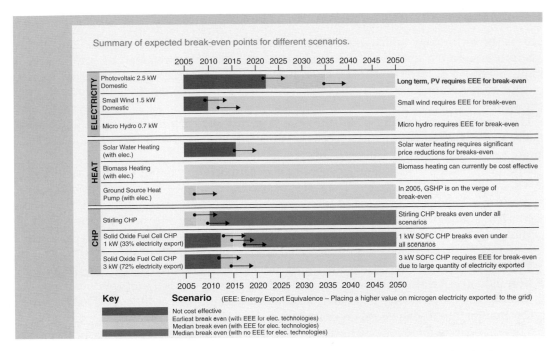

Figure 9.1   Current, medium and long-term prospects for microgeneration technologies (courtesy of the Energy Saving Trust)

- Small-scale power has a short lead time and can be planned, built and commissioned in a much shorter time than is the case with larger plants.
- It can obviate the need for new large-scale power plants often subject to public enquiry. This is especially important in the case of new nuclear installations.
- Micropower is capable of running on a variety of fuels emitting rates of particulates, sulphur dioxide, nitrogen oxides and carbon dioxide which are significantly lower than larger plants. In the case of direct hydrogen, this means zero emissions.
- It is largely immune to the price volatility of fossil fuels distributed by the large utilities, a fact that will be increasingly advantageous as oil and gas prices reflect diminishing reserves or political tensions.
- There can be community control and choice of the technology. This can trigger local initiatives like a plant for the treatment of sewage through anaerobic digestion to produce biogas for the energy system.

The shift to distributed or embedded generation is part of a trend which was first witnessed in computers. Mainframe and minicomputers were all but vanquished by the personal computer, just as the fixed telephone has been severely challenged by the mobile phone and email.

The virtue of a distributed system is endorsed by the Washington Worldwatch Institute, which states: 'An electricity grid with many small generators is inherently more stable than a grid serviced by only a few large plants. So-called intelligent grids which can receive as well as distribute electricity at every node are already emerging.' Seth Dunn of the Washington Worldwatch Institute believes that micropower is the shape of the future for energy: 'It is not inconceivable that, in the long run, most of society's power will come from small-scale local systems, with the rest coming from large wind farms and solar plants making centralized thermal plants no longer necessary'.[1]

Microturbines

This is the technology which looks set to penetrate the US market at a phenomenal rate. Microturbines are a spin-off from the jet engine industry. Heat released by combustion at high-speed drives turbine blades that, in turn, spin a high speed generator. Their power output ranges from 15 to 300 kW. If their waste heat is usefully employed they are highly efficient.

Having only two moving parts, they are straightforward to manufacture and consequently relatively cheap. Maintenance is kept to a minimum since no lubricants or coolants are required. Their life expectancy is about 40,000 hours.

Another benefit is that turbines can use a variety of fuels, for example, natural gas, propane, kerosene, diesel fuel and biogas. The last is of particular interest since anaerobic digestion processing of biological waste to produce biogas may become increasingly popular.

It is a technology that is especially suitable for the domestic and small business market. Groups of homes needing between 25 kW and 300 kW of power will be obvious candidates for microturbines, especially with their CHP/cogeneration potential.

The US producer of microturbines, Capstone, predicted that by ~2007 this will be a $1 billion industry. Assuming the economy of scale of at least 100,000 units per year, a 30 kW turbine would cost $400/kW. Ultimately a 100 kW unit could cost as little as $200/kW, which is less than half that of the most economic conventional power plants.

There are reservations about microturbines for individual homes. They can be scaled down appropriately but the main problem is that they require a pressurized gas supply which raises safety concerns within homes. A small leak could lead to an explosion.

Fuel cells

As indicated on p. 83 and Fig. 7.5, an innovative UK fuel cell company, Ceres Power, is focusing on mini-fuel cells from 1 to 10 kW output. The company has linked up with British Gas to provide a 1 kW fuel cell to heat a domestic boiler and provide electricity simultaneously. It is a solid oxide fuel cell operating at about 600°C. Because of its high operating temperature the cell is able to run directly off natural gas, hence the interest shown by British Gas. It takes some time to reach its operating temperature but this should not be a problem in a static situation. A fuel cell in this range of output could be destined to revolutionize the domestic energy market, especially as homes become more efficient at retaining warmth. The long-term value of this system lies in the fact that this type of fuel cell will still be appropriate as and when the full-blown hydrogen economy becomes established. It should be market-ready by 2007.

Stirling combined heat and power

The alternative system that is already on the market is a micro-CHP (combined heat and power) unit based on the Stirling engine. The UK government is increasingly promoting micro-CHP as part of its strategy to reduce CO_2 emissions, especially in the domestic sector.

It is interesting how two nineteenth century technologies, the fuel cell and the Stirling engine, are only now coming into their own. Invented by Robert Stirling in 1816, the eponymous machine is an 'external combustion engine' because the heat is applied to the outside of the cylinder. It is a viable technology because of advances in piston technology and in materials like ceramics from the space industry and high-temperature steels, allowing temperatures to rise to 1200°C. It is now considered a firm contender for the small-scale micropower market.

The operational principle of the Stirling engine is that a fixed amount of gas is sealed within the chamber of the engine, usually helium, nitrogen or hydrogen. The Stirling engine works on the basis that when heated the gas will expand. Heat is applied to one end of the chamber using a possible variety of fuels to 750–800°C. The increased pressure within the cylinder forces down the power piston. In the basic design a second element, the displacer piston, seals off the hot end of the engine, forcing the gas into a water-cooled chamber. Here the gas contracts, drawing the piston back to the top of its stroke, compressing the gas in the process ready to be heated for the next power stroke. The displacer piston then seals off the cool end of the system.

There are two basic types of Stirling engine:

- where the linear action of the pistons is converted to rotary motion to power a generator
- hermetically sealed free piston Stirling engines (FPSE) in which electricity is produced by an alternator within the sealed chamber.

The first type comes in three configurations: *alpha, beta*, and *gamma*.

Alpha Stirling engine

This operates with two separate power cylinders, one 'hot' and the other 'cold'. As it implies, the former sits within the high-temperature heat exchanger and the cold inside the cooling heat exchanger. The four-phase cycle is illustrated in Figs 9.2 to 9.5.

Commercial Stirling units often have a multicylinder configuration which dispenses with the displacer piston. Four cylinders are arranged axially and connected to a 'swash plate' or 'Wobble yoke' (WhisperGen) that converts the linear action to rotary drive for three-phase electricity generators. The reciprocating motion of any two cylinders is 90 degrees opposed. The expansion space of the cylinders is maintained at high temperature by the constant combustion of fuel via heating tubes. The compression spaces are kept constantly water-cooled. A third heat exchanger is the regenerator positioned alongside the cylinders. This absorbs heat and then returns it to the hydrogen thereby improving energy efficiency (see Fig. 9.6).

For some years the market in the UK has been dominated by WhisperTech, a New Zealand company marketing the 'WhisperGen' domestic CHP system. It provides domestic hot water and space heating along with electricity. It produces 5 kW of usable heat and ~800 W of electricity.

As there is no combustion stage, this particular Stirling engine is relatively quiet in operation, producing 44 dBA at 7 m. It is this characteristic which made it popular for operation within submarines where sometimes silence is golden. This is also a feature which makes it ideal as a replacement for a conventional domestic boiler. It does not require lubricants and servicing need only occur about every 10,000 hours. It is normally linked to a conventional independently heated boiler.

The US manufacturer STM Power (Stirling Thermal Motors) produces engines with a capacity of 55 kilowatts of electricity for small commercial premises and groups of domestic properties. With heat derived from biogas from landfill or anaerobic digestion it is as near carbon neutral as is possible. STM Power claims 30% electrical efficiency and a total efficiency of 80% in CHP application (see Figs 9.7 and 9.8).

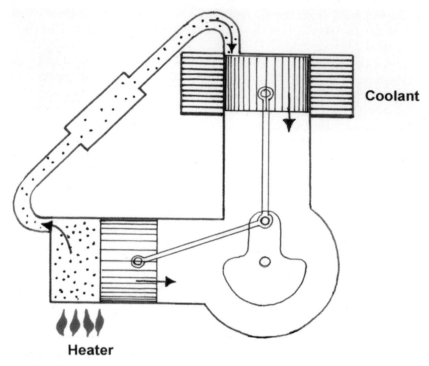

Figure 9.2 At the first stage the gas has been driven into the hot chamber, where it is heated and expands causing the pistons to move inwards (courtesy of Wikipedia)

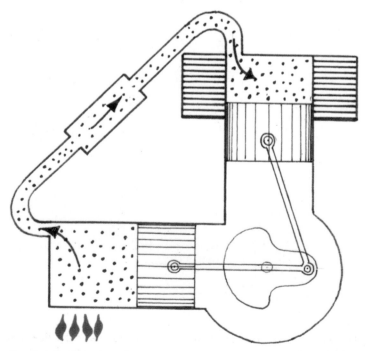

Figure 9.3 The flywheel effect then drives the crankshaft through 90 degrees, thereby transferring most of the gas to the cool cylinder (courtesy of Wikipedia)

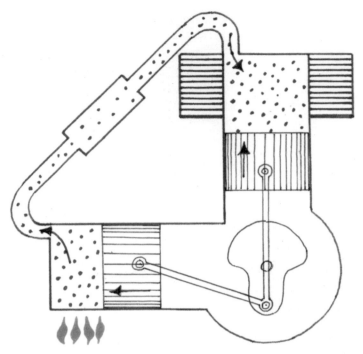

Figure 9.4   In the third phase the gas, now in the cool cylinder, contracts, pulling both pistons outwards (courtesy of Wikipedia)

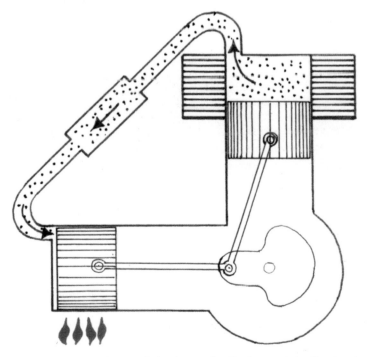

Figure 9.5   In the fourth phase, the gas is in the cool cylinder, and the flywheel momentum helps move the crank through 90 degrees, transferring the gas to the hot cylinder for the process to begin again (courtesy of Wikipedia)

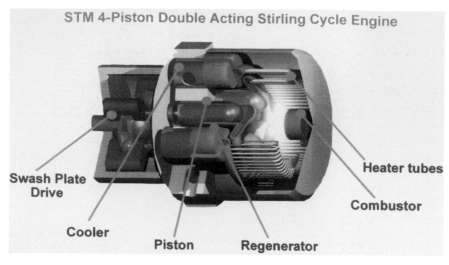

Figure 9.6   Axial configuration of cylinders (courtesy of STM Power)

Beta Stirling Engine

This has a single power piston in the same cylinder and on the same shaft as a displacer piston. The latter is a loose fit piston which serves to move the working gas from the hot zone to the cold heat exchanger. As the working gas is pushed to the hot zone of the cylinder it expands and pushes down the power piston. At the cold end the gas contracts and the momentum of the flywheel helps push the power piston to the hot whilst also compressing the gas. Figure 9.9 is a diagrammatic representation of the system.

Gamma Stirling engine

This is a variation on the beta engine in which the power piston is in a separate cylinder alongside a cylinder accommodating the displacer piston but sharing a common flywheel. The gas flows freely between the two cylinders. This arrangement is often used in multicylinder engines.

Free piston Stirling engines (FPSE)

The second main category of Stirling engine is a version in which the piston floats freely within a hermetically sealed cylinder thus without an external linkage to drive a generator. This elegant development of the Stirling principle is even more silent than the previous examples and is ideal for domestic use. Sunpower Inc., a US company, plans to introduce a system to the UK in 2007 which is based on a Stirling engine which incorporates an alternator within the cylinder which produces 1 kW of electricity at 50 cycles. This makes it compatible with the grid. The top of the cylinder is heated in the conventional way. The base is cooled by return water from a radiator system which is sufficiently cool to create the pressure difference needed to power the piston. It will be marketed in the UK by Microgen and promises to be an attractive alternative to a conventional domestic boiler (see Fig. 9.10).

The UK is a particularly favourable market for this technology for several reasons:

- A high proportion of households are owner-occupied.
- Of the 22 million or so gas consumers, over 14 million have central heating and rising. This is essential to absorb the heat dumped into the cooling water.

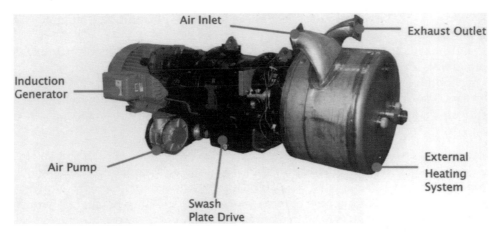

Figure 9.7 The components of the 565 kW STM Stirling CHP unit (courtesy of STM Power)

Figure 9.8 The STM unit in situ (courtesy of STM Power)

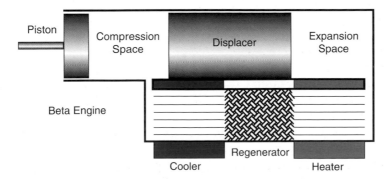

Figure 9.9 Principle of the single cylinder beta Stirling engine

- All consumers are linked to a reliable grid electricity supply, necessary to import power when necessary.
- The ratio of heat demand to electricity demand in a typical house is ~5:1, which is compatible with the heat-to-electricity ratio output of the Stirling engine.
- As an addition to a conventional central heating boiler the target pay-back time is 3–4 years. This may reduce as the price of gas and electricity continues to rise.
- Microgen claim that, if every suitable home in the UK used this technology, it would reduce its CO_2 emissions by 25%.

Sunpower Inc. is also currently developing a four cylinder free piston engine linked to a gas turbine output stage. The pistons are connected to gas compressors. The compressors are then used to drive a gas turbine. The prototype machine uses double acting compressors so that the turbine receives eight pulses of energy for each cycle of the engine. This promises to be a low-maintenance, high-reliability technology, mainly due to the absence of heavily loaded moving parts.

Another application of Stirling technology is being researched in The Netherlands. This links the FPSE to a groundwater source heat pump to become the free piston Stirling heat pump (FPSHP). It is a hermetically sealed system in which the mechanical output of the FPSE using helium is directly connected to a Rankine cycle heat pump using CO_2 as its working gas. The alternator within the FPSE powers components such as the water circulation pump, indoor fan, burner blower and electronics. The system will supply heat for

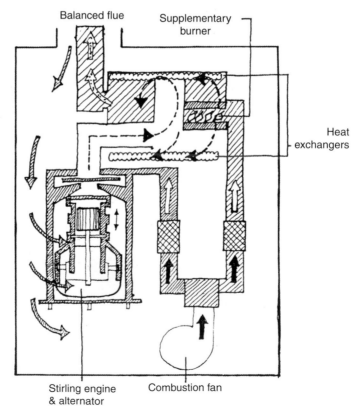

Figure 9.10   Sunpower/Microgen free piston domestic Stirling CHP unit

domestic hot water, and space heating. It will be capable of operating in either heating or cooling mode.[2]

To summarize the benefits of the Stirling engine:

- it can use any combustible fuel from agricultural and forestry waste to biogas and natural gas
- it is up to 80% efficient when used for CHP
- it is robust, being of simple construction and requiring low maintenance
- it is quiet running, which makes it suitable for domestic application
- it is durable, offering up to 60,000 hours of life
- it is competitively priced compared with conventional boilers, taking into account the electricity generation.

Later in the decade it is possible that the Stirling engine will play a significant part in the shift to combined heat and power in the domestic sector. This is because it is one of the few CHP units presently available which can be scaled down to suit an individual house. The Microgen FPSE 'personal CHP' can be wall-mounted to produce up to 15 kW of heat as well as 1 kW of electricity.

According to MicroGen the estimated average cost saving in electricity was £200 per year in 2003. Since then electricity prices have risen considerably. Hopefully the UK government will sanction the widespread adoption of net metering on a one-for-one basis as a way of promoting microgeneration. Only then will householders get a fair deal for their home produced electricity. The situation should be helped when the whole of the EU has liberalized the electricity market by 2010 at the latest.

Notes

1. Quoted in *Renewable Energy World*, November/December 2000
2. David Berchowitz, Director and Yong-Rak Kwon, Senior Engineer Global Cooling BV Ijsselburcht 3, 6825 BS Arnhem, The Netherlands

10 Small-scale hydro

Hydropower has a history going back at least 2000 years. The Doomsday book records 5000 waterwheels. One of the earliest hydroelectric schemes and first in the world to power a private home was installed by the First Lord Armstrong in the 1880s at Cragside in Northumberland. This means, of course, that it is not exactly at the cutting edge of progress. The expansion of the National Grid sounded the death knell for many small hydroschemes. However, it is increasingly now being perceived as an important source of clean electricity, devoid of the environmental penalties associated with large-scale hydropower. It has minimal impact on the environment, resulting in almost zero emissions of SO_2, CO_2 and NOx. Nor does it cause acidification of water; on the contrary, it can oxygenate rivers and streams.

A life-cycle comparison with coal and combined cycle natural gas makes the point (see Table 10.1).

Renewable energy systems have 31 times less impact on the environment than fossil-based energy, with one kWh produced by small-scale hydro being 300 times less polluting than the dirtiest of them all, lignite.

Another method of comparison is to award ecopoints to the various technologies. These are points of environmental penalty. The factors considered include global warming, ozone depletion, acidification, eutrophication of water, heavy metal pollution, emission of carcinogens, production of winter and summer smog, industrial waste, radioactive waste and radioactivity and depletion of energy resources.

Table 10.2 compares small hydro with other energy sources on this basis.

According to a European Union White Paper *A Community Strategy and Action Plan for the Future: Renewable Sources of Energy* (November 1997), 'only about 20% of the economic potential for small hydro power plants has so far been exploited . . . An additional installed capacity of 4500 MW of small hydro plants by 2010 is a realistic contribution which could be achieved.'

Table 10.1 Life cycle emissions g/kWh

	CO_2	SO_2	NOx
Small hydro	3.6–11.6	0.009–0.024	0.003–0.006
Natural gas combined cycle	402	0.2	0.3
Coal	1026	1.2	1.8

Table 10.2   Comparative eco-penalty points

Fuel	Ecopoints
Fuel oil	1398
Coal	1356
Nuclear	672
Natural gas	267
Small hydro	5

Source: APPA (Spain) Study on Environmental Impact of the Production of Electricity.

The Community guidelines also recognize the need to internalize the external costs of electricity generation. Investments in renewables are deemed to be equivalent to environmental investments.

Having said all this, there is a sting in the tail. The European Commission does *not* consider that small hydro should receive support as a source of renewable energy. This is because it reckons that large-scale hydro can produce electricity at market prices. Small hydro suffers because of this blanket perception. It also reveals that the Commission is still driven by market rather than environmental considerations since small hydro is one of the cleanest of all technologies as stated above.

As for defining small-hydro, the EU regards 10 MW as the demarcation line. There are two ways of extracting energy from situations capable of providing a head of water. They both depend on geographical/geological characteristics and the location of a suitable water source.

- Mountainous country provides a high hydraulic head of water which makes a high-speed impulse turbine the appropriate conversion technology.
- River valleys usually only create opportunities for a low head of water, generally less than 20 m. In this case water is diverted to a pipe (penstock) or channel (leat) leading to a crossflow turbine like an updated water wheel or a Kaplan turbine which has variable blades. Turbines are now available which can exploit as little as 2–3 m head of water.

The essential components of a hydro scheme are:

- an adequate rainfall catchment area
- a weir or dam to provide a suitable head of water
- alternatively, a river with a suitable drop in level to enable water to be diverted to a penstock or leat to be delivered to a turbine at the right speed and in the right quantity
- a turbine, generator and electrical connection
- a tailrace to return water to the river.

One of the concerns about this technology is that it can deplete fish stocks. Some reports implicate small hydro in the destruction of salmon fishing in a part of Spain. The remedy is a fish channel suitable for even the smallest fish incorporating an acoustic guidance system to prevent fish entering the forebay of the plant. An alternative is an electric fish screen which was first tested at a 500 kW installation at Deanston, Scotland.

In the UK the most abundant small hydro potential is in Scotland. An example of a community initiative to harness small hydro energy is the 230 kW scheme at Loch Poll within the North Assynt Estate in Sutherland. The Assynt Crofters' Trust constructed a dam to raise the

Figure 10.1   Ffestiniog small hydroplant, Tanygrisiau, North Wales

level of the loch. Water channelled along a penstock drives a turbine-driven generator which produces around 1.32 GWh of electricity per year. The Trust has a 15-year contract to sell to the grid. This is the most northerly hydroelectric project in the UK and has been the basis of a study into the provision of small hydro serving remote communities.

A 200 kW turbine has been constructed at a weir on the River Thames. This location is important since it will raise the profile of small hydro within the metropolitan field of influence.

How discreet small hydro can be within an area of outstanding beauty such as the Snowdonia National Park is illustrated by the Garnedd power station near Dolwyddelan, North Wales. It is a run-of-river scheme which taps the energy from the Tyn-y-ddol river. Water is fed into a penstock pipe from a small pond 1 km from the plant and with a static head of 102 metres.

A Turgo impulse turbine drives a synchronous generator producing up to 600 kW and an average of 2.3 GW/h per year. The power station is operated and monitored remotely.

Similarly discreet is the small hydro plant at Tanygrisiau, which discharges its tail race into the lake which serves the pump storage for Ffestiniog power station (see Fig. 10.1).

One of the most cost effective ways of installing small hydro is to restore the infrastructure created for industrial water power, usually in eighteenth- and nineteenth-century mills.

A successful run-of-river low-head project has been in operation at Blantyre Mill on the River Clyde since 1995. With an output of 576 kW it supplies the grid under contract. The site has a 200-year tradition of exploiting water power for a cotton mill later to become a sawmill. Salmon have been returning to the Clyde and so a by-pass channel for the fish is incorporated into the scheme.

Occasionally older hydropower plants have been abandoned as grid-delivered power became economically attractive. Now things have gone full circle and hydroinstallations are being refurbished. An example is the East Mill in Belper, Derbyshire, a low head run-of-river scheme linked to a weir.

Micro-hydro

Despite often having access to wind or hydropower, about two billion people or one third of the earth's population have no electricity. Many small communities, especially in the developing world, do not have the resources to embark on a small hydro project, but *micro-hydro* is another matter. It covers systems providing between 10 and 100 kW of power. A typical case is the Vavanga Community, a village on the south west coast of Kolombangara Island, one of the Solomon Islands. It now has electricity thanks to Appropriate Technology for Community and Environment (APACE) based in NSW Australia, a non-profit community-based agency assisting overseas communities to engage in sustainable development.

The system consists of a timber weir feeding a four-pipe penstock which powers a turbine serving a 240 V AC synchronous generator with an output of 4–7 kW, depending on the season. The power is fed to the village 2 km away by a combination of underground and overhead cable. In the first instance 22 houses, 14 kitchens, two church premises and a bakery were connected to the supply. Typically two 18 W fluorescent lights and one power point are served in each household. To ensure that the river can supply an equitable amount of power when rates of flow vary, a current-limiting device is installed in each household. However, community facilities and businesses receive unlimited power.

Villagers took an active part in the installation of the project. As a run-of-river scheme it is mechanically relatively straightforward, which has enabled the villagers to be trained to carry out routine maintenance (see Fig. 10.2). Oversight is provided by APACE, which liaises with the community hydro committee regarding local resource utilization, local distribution and the design of buildings.

Figure 10.2 Villagers maintaining the plant (courtesy of Caddet)

The electrification of Vavanga and similar villages has a variety of positive impacts, not least the fact that it has slowed the population migration from villages to towns. There is now better village welfare. New homes are being built that are connected to the supply. There is a new church. Existing homes are being repaired and well maintained. There is street lighting.

The community plans to upgrade the system, first by replacing the timber weir with a concrete structure; and then by tapping an additional tributary of the river with a second penstock feeding a small turbine.

The cause of micro-hydro has recently been further advanced by the development of a 'power controller' by a Danish engineer, Steen Carlsen. This makes it possible to create stand-alone power plants much more cheaply. It supplies AC current to a quality matching that from a large public grid and at a price that is a mere fraction of that from traditional synchronous generators previously necessary for stand-alone plants. The device provides a fixed voltage within a margin of 1%. This has an impact on the life of light bulbs for example. If a filament bulb receives an excess voltage of 10% its life expectancy is reduced by 70%. In developing countries this is an important consideration. Another problem with isolated off-grid communities is that they have a problem with surplus electricity.

A village in the Peruvian Andes was the first to receive the power controller. The device maintains a steady three-phase output from a turbine-driven asynchronous motor by diverting surplus power to a heating cartridge (a large immersion heater) in a central tank which can distribute hot water to the community (see Fig. 10.3).

A further trick of the power controller is that it can 'deceive' conventional electric motors into acting as though they were connected to the grid. This allows cheap standard electric motors to be used as generators, enabling wind or hydro schemes to operate in either stand-alone or grid-connected mode.

The fact that the inhabitants can now heat their homes and domestic water from the micro-hydro source has meant that they are no longer reliant on wood from the surrounding

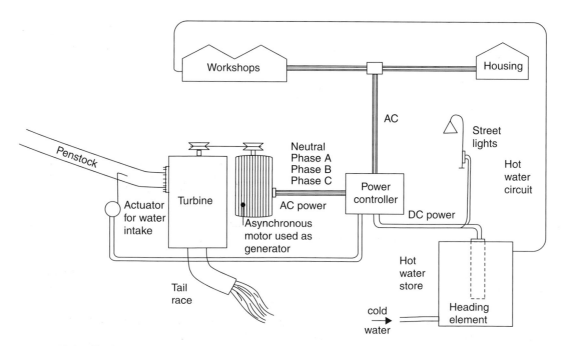

Figure 10.3   Typical village system with power controller

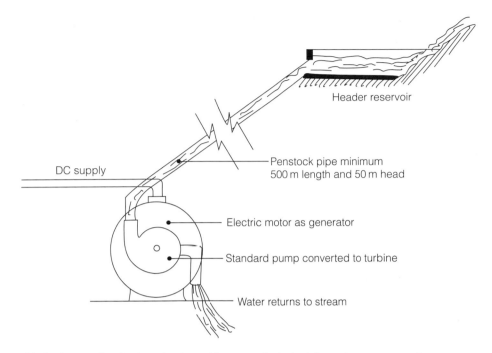

Header reservoir

DC supply

Penstock pipe minimum
500 m length and 50 m head

Electric motor as generator

Standard pump converted to turbine

Water returns to stream

Figure 10.4   Improvised micro-hydro with converted electric motor as generator

forests. So, it is countering 'survival' deforestation and the erosion of soil which accompanies it. It is also providing power for small-scale industries and workshops, further placing a brake on the drift to the cities.

Finally, a Yorkshire farmer, Bill Cowperthwaite, has demonstrated how micro-hydro can come within the DIY range. His ideas have been adopted by the charity Intermediate Technology. The principle is to use components which are cheap and readily available in developing countries. What is required is a length of metal or PVC pipe for the penstock, a standard pump, and an electric motor. The pump is converted into a turbine by reversing the connections. If pumps are not available Intermediate Technology has devised a programme for teaching villagers how to fabricate turbines from waste metal. The electric motor can be converted into a generator. Electric motors work by generating an electric field within the motor which causes a magnet at the core of the motor to spin. Generators work in reverse by spinning the central magnet, causing current to flow to the external electromagnet. Capacitors are all that are required to convert the motors into generators. These store electricity for the short time required to even out the variations in voltage as the core rotates. It is reckoned that the cost of an electric motor and converting it to work as a generator is significantly less than the cost of a purpose-built generator for rating up to 20 kW. There is a bonus in that electric motors generally have heavier bearings than commercial generators, giving them a life expectancy of at least 10 years (see Fig. 10.4).

The final piece of the kit is an electric controller which manages the flow of electricity. As in the Peruvian scheme the controller directs electricity which is temporarily surplus to demand to a heat sink. The controllers can be made locally and are already being manufactured in numerous rural sites, for example in Nepal.

Whilst small hydro has considerable potential in the industrialized countries, micro-hydro in association with other compact renewable technologies raises the possibility of transforming the lives of rural communities in developing countries.

11 Wave and tide

Wave power is a fairly high density form of solar energy since the winds that generate waves are created by heat from solar radiation. Solar power can be transformed into waves with an energy density of 100 kW per metre length of wave crest. The World Energy Council estimates that wave power could meet 10% of world electricity demand. It is regarded as a reliable power source and has been estimated as being capable of meeting 25% or ~12 GW of peak UK demand. With an estimated load factor of 50% for wave power this suggests a reliable output of ~6 GW.

The sea is, in effect, a huge mass-spring system which oscillates with a fixed frequency. The average wave length is around 120 m and, in high seas, a wave carries about 100 kW/m of potential energy to be captured by a variety of technologies.

Point absorbers

As the term suggests, these are systems which are focused on a nodal form of absorbing the energy of the waves to generate electricity. One technology which is on the verge of being market ready is the Interproject Service (IPS) Offshore Wave Energy Converter (OWEC) system. This uses only wave energy and is not affected by tidal or ocean currents (see Fig. 11.1).

The system consists of a floating buoy (A) attached to the sea bed by 'elastic' moorings enabling it to exploit the motion of the waves. The buoy height is 5–6 metres with a diameter of 5–10 metres and requires a water depth of 40–50 metres. Attached to the buoy is a vertical tube or 'acceleration tube' (B) of a length around three times the diameter of the buoy up to 25 m. Within the acceleration tube there is a free moving piston (C) which has a restricted stroke to prevent overloading of the system.

The principle is that the buoy moves vertically against the damping mass of the water in the acceleration tube under the buoy. The relative movement between the buoy and the water mass in the tube is transferred by the piston (D) into the energy conversion system consisting of a hydraulic pumping cylinder which, via a hydraulic motor, drives the generator (E). The OWEC converts 30–35% of the energy of the waves into electricity. It is suggested that there would be clusters of units making up a complete power plant which could generate over 200 kW.

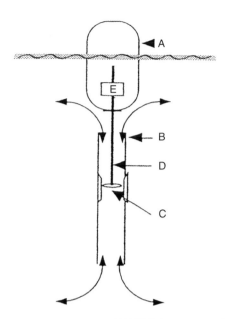

Figure 11.1   Offshore Wave Energy Converter (OWEC) (courtesy of Interproject Services)

The Danish Maritime Institute has developed another form of point absorber which also employs a float connected by a polyester rope to a suction cup anchor. The rope is attached to a hydraulic actuator within the float which pumps fluid into a high pressure hydraulic accumulator. The return stroke is provided by a hydraulic fluid from a low-pressure accumulator. As waves create motion in the float, a pressure difference between the high and low pressure accumulators builds up. The pressure difference drives a hydraulic motor and generator. A system with a 5–6 m diameter would have a rated output of 20–30 kW. The ultimate objective is to construct a 10 m buoy with an output of around 120 kW (see Fig. 11.2).

A variation on the theme has been developed by the Energy Centre of The Netherlands (ECN). It is called the Archimedes Wave Swing and consists of a number of air-filled chambers below the surface of the sea. Above these are movable floats in the form of hoods which oscillate vertically with the pressure created by the wave motion. These would be about 20 m in diameter and weigh roughly 1000 tonnes. The top of each float is shaped like a funnel which maximizes the point absorbing effect. As a wave crest moves over the hood, the internal pressure rises. The trapped air is pushed into another chamber and the hood begins its descent. The process is reversed in a wave trough. The vertical motion is converted to rotary action to drive a generator. The system is positioned about 20 m below the surface with the float designed to be in balance with that amount of water above it. At this depth the system is protected from damage from extreme storms (see Fig. 11.3).

The intention is that groups of three floats will be connected so that as a wave progresses it creates a succession of oscillations. It is reckoned that a three-chamber unit will produce about 2.7 MW.

The first successful shore-based wave energy device in the UK was installed on the Isle of Islay in the north of Scotland. It was designed by The Queen's University, Belfast, and it works on the principle of the oscillating water column (OWC). Incoming waves enter a concrete chamber and force air into a turbine linked to a generator. The outgoing wave sucks air back through the turbine which is designed to rotate in the same direction under both circumstances. This patented system is called a Wells Turbine. This prototype generated

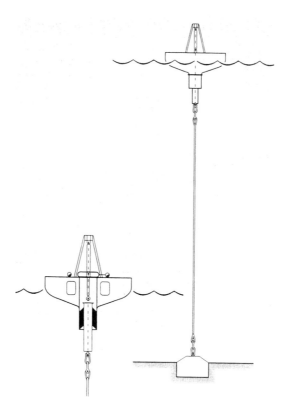

Figure 11.2   Danish Point Absorber (courtesy of Caddet)

75 kW which went directly to the Grid. Following the success of the prototype, a larger scale version called The Limpet was installed with a capacity of ~450 kW (see Fig. 11.4).

At Port Kembla in Australia a wave energy device which is a variation on the oscillating water column (OCW) principle is now operational. It was designed to be installed against the sea side of harbour walls or rocky peninsulas where there is deep water. A parabola-shaped wave concentrator extends into the sea, amplifying the waves by a factor of three by the time they reach the focal point. There they enter an air-filled chamber, forcing the air forwards and drawing it backwards through an aperture leading to a turbine as the waves arrive and then retreat. The angle of the turbine blades is adjusted via a sensor system so that they rotate in the same direction regardless of the direction of the air flow. This involves a pressure transducer which measures the pressure exerted on the ocean floor by each wave as it enters the chamber. A voltage signal proportional to the pressure is sent to a program-mable logic controller (PLC) indicating the height and duration of each wave. The PLC adjusts the blade angle through a series of pinions and planet gears. A motion software program ensures that the information from the pressure transducer is translated into the optimal blade position at any given moment (see Fig. 11.5).

The Port Kembla installation has a peak capacity 500 kW and an output of over 1 GWh/year which is fed to the grid. The economics of the system compare favourably with solar energy and wind power. With refinements to the system the unit price is expected to outclass all competitors. A single installation of this kind has the potential to generate 1000 kW which would power 2000 homes (Caddet). Several sites in Australia such as the Bass Strait and Southern Australia coast have the wave potential to generate up to 1 MW per unit.

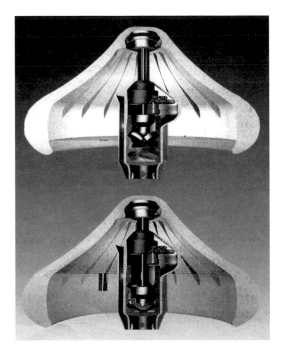

Figure 11.3   Archimedes hoods in the raised and lowered positions (courtesy of Caddet)

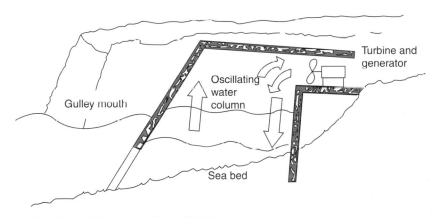

Figure 11.4   Principle of the Isle of Islay OWC wave generator

In the right location, wave energy is more consistent and thus less intermittent energy source than either wind or solar. It causes no pollution and by offsetting the fossil generation saved by the plant, the savings in CO_2 are around 790 tonnes/year.

Currently under test in the Orkneys is a snake-like device called Pelamis, which consists of five flexibly linked floating cylinders, each of 3.5 m diameter (see Fig. 11.6). The joints between the cylinders contain pumps which force oil through hydraulic electricity generators in response to the rise and fall of the waves. It is estimated to produce 750 kW of electricity. The manufacturer, Ocean Power Devices (OPD), claims that a 30 MW wave farm covering a square kilometre of sea would provide power for 20,000 homes. Twenty such farms would provide enough electricity for a city the size of Edinburgh. The first commercial Pelamis wave farm is

Figure 11.5   Wave generator, Port Kembla installation (courtesy of Caddet)

Figure 11.6   The Pelamis demonstration machine (courtesy of Ocean Power Delivery Ltd)

being installed off the Portuguese northern coast. It consists of three P-750 units rated at 2.5 MW installed capacity. The Portuguese government has also issued a letter of intent to order a further 30 Pelamis machines subject to the satisfactory performance of the first project.

The UK and Portugal are currently the focus of wave power investment due both to their geography and to the subsidies available for demonstration projects.

Like Scotland, Norway enjoys an enormous potential for extracting energy from waves. As far back as 1986 a demonstration ocean wave power plant was built based on the 'Tapchan' concept (see Fig. 11.7). This consists of a 60-metre long tapering channel built within an inlet to the sea. The narrowing channel has the effect of amplifying the wave height. This lifts the sea water about 4 metres depositing it into a 7500 m^2 reservoir. The head of water is sufficient to operate a conventional hydroelectric power plant with a capacity of 370 kW.

A large-scale version of this concept is under construction on the south coast of Java in association with the Norwegians. The plant will have a capacity of 1.1 MW. As a system this has numerous advantages:

- the conversion device is passive with no moving parts in the open sea
- the Tapchan plant is able to cope with extremes of weather

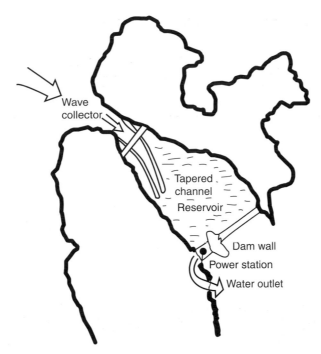

Figure 11.7   Wave elevator system, the Tapchan

- the main mechanical components are standard products of proven reliability
- maintenance costs are very low
- the plant is totally pollution free
- it is unobtrusive
- it will produce cheap electricity for remote islands.

Large-scale tidal energy

The tidal barrage

Trapping water at high tide and releasing it when there is an adequate head is an ancient technology. A medieval tide mill is still in working order in Woodbridge, Suffolk. In the first quarter of the last century this principle was applied to electricity generation in the feasibility studies for a barrage across the River Severn.

Tidal power works on the principle that water is held back on the ebb tide to provide a sufficient head of water to rotate a turbine. Dual generation is possible if the flow tide is also exploited. However, this has the disadvantage that the turbines are less efficient, having to cater for two-directional flow. Also the changing from flow to ebb generation means that the turbines cannot exploit the full tidal range.

The only operational barrage in Europe is at La Rance, Normandy. It was designed in the 1960s with a capacity of 240 MW, giving an annual production of about 610 gigawatt hours (GWh). Despite some mechanical problems in 1975 the scheme has been a success. Even so, the French government elected to concentrate its generation policy on nuclear power which accounts for about 75% of its capacity (see Figs 11.8 and 11.9).

The technology of barrages was transformed by the caisson techniques employed in the construction of the Mulberry Harbour floated into place after D-Day in World War II. It is a

Figure 11.8   Tidal barrage, La Rance, Normandy

Figure 11.9   Tidal barrage and turbine hall, La Rance, Normandy

modular technique with turbine caissons constructed on slipways or temporary sand islands. The Energy Technology Support Unit (ETSU) stated in 1992: 'The UK has, probably the most favourable conditions in Europe for generating electricity from the tides'. In fact, it has about half all the European Union's tidal generating potential of about 105 terawatt

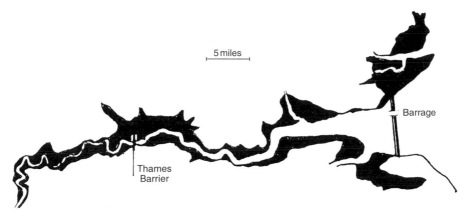

Figure 11.10   Thames valley below 5 metres with proposed barrage

hours per year (TWh/y). The report concludes:

> *There are several advantages arising from the construction of tidal barrages in addition to providing a clean, non-polluting source of energy. Tidal barrages can assist with the local infrastructure of the region, create regional development opportunities and provide protection against local flooding within the basin during storm surge.*[1]

Around the world the estimated potential for capturing tidal energy is about 1000 GW. However, constraints like access to construction sites and centres of population or a national grid reduce the realistic potential to around 100 GW.[2]

One of the best tidal opportunities exists in Canada in the Bay of Fundy where there is a proposal to generate 6400 MW. China has 500 possible sites with a total capacity of 110.0 GW. In the UK the longest running debate about tidal energy has centred on the River Severn estuary. It is still no nearer realization despite the fact that it has a potential capacity of 8.6 GW. However, its load factor of 23% (the proportion of rated power actually delivered to the grid) means that its realistic capacity is about 2 GW.

The most pressing case for a hard barrage in the UK is located in the Thames estuary. It is a situation identified by the Met Office as being the most vulnerable in northern Europe to severe storm surges up to and beyond 2080. Especially threatened would be the proposed Thames Gateway housing development. A tidal barrage would also be able to generate considerable quantities of electricity via underwater turbines and 5 MW wind turbines along its apex (see Fig. 11.10).

In the 1970s and 1980s one of the arguments against tidal barrages was that they would trap pollution upstream. Since rivers are now appreciably cleaner in Europe than in the 1970s thanks largely to EU directives, this should not now be a factor. The Thames is claimed to be the cleanest river in Europe, playing host to salmon and other desirable fish species. A group of engineering companies has renewed the argument in favour of the River Severn barrage, indicating that it would meet 6% of Britain's electricity needs whilst protecting the estuary's coastline from flooding.[3]

Offshore impoundment

An alternative to estuary tidal generation is the concept of the tidal pound. The idea is not new as mentioned earlier. The system is ideal for situations in which there is a significant tidal range and shallow tidal flats encountered in many coasts of the UK. The system consists

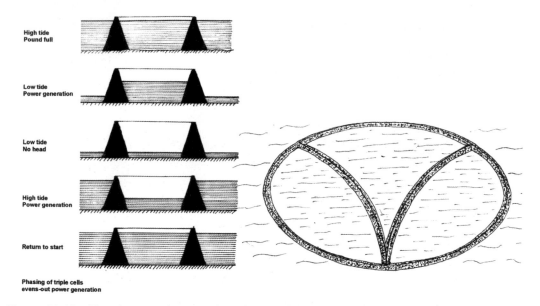

High tide
Pound full

Low tide
Power generation

Low tide
No head

High tide
Power generation

Return to start

Phasing of triple cells
evens-out power generation

Figure 11.11   The shape and generating phases of tidal impoundment

of an oval barrage built from locally sourced loose rock, sand and gravel similar in appearance to standard coastal defences. It is divided into three or more segments to allow for the phasing of supply to match demand. According to Tidal Electricity Ltd., computer simulations show that a load factor of 62% can be achieved with generation possible 81% of the time. Tidal pounds would be fitted with low-head tidal generating equipment that is a reliable and mature technology (see Fig. 11.11).

There is a technology which overcomes most of the problems associated with barrage schemes whilst generating power on an equivalent scale. It is known as the 'tidal energy bridge' or 'tidal fence' which can be conceived as a bridge with numerous supports. Vertical axis turbines are contained within a concrete structure which allows the free flow of water at all times. The bridge structure reduces the cross-sectional area of an estuary location, thereby increasing the rate of flow by up to a factor of four. It is a system as efficient in tidal streams and coastal currents as on an estuary site. The UK is one of the most favoured of all locations in this respect. Of all the renewable technologies, large-scale tidal is one of the most likely candidates as a substitute for a new generation of nuclear plants. Spread round the most suitable locations with varying tide times this system could provide reliable base load electricity for an electricity infrastructure which will become increasingly reliant on intermittent suppliers (see Fig. 11.12). The prime candidate is the Seven estuary.

Tidal currents

Whereas the tidal fence is appropriate for capturing fast tidal flow between land masses like an estuary or well-defined channel, other technologies can exploit the energy content of tidal currents that oscillate along coasts. These have to be distinguished from large ocean movements like the Gulf Stream, which are thermodynamic phenomena.

Horizontal-axis underwater turbines are the favoured technology for offshore tidal currents. They are similar to wind turbines but water has an energy density four times greater than air, which means that a rotor 15 m in diameter will generate as much power as a wind

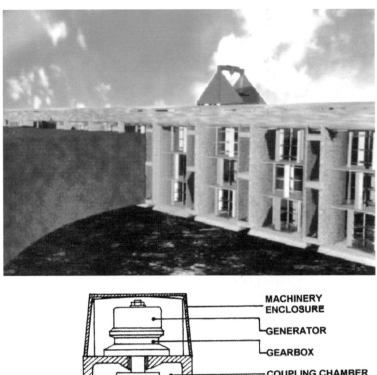

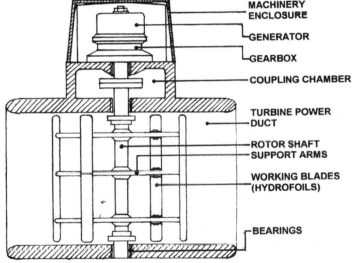

MACHINERY
ENCLOSURE

GENERATOR

GEARBOX

COUPLING CHAMBER

TURBINE POWER
DUCT

ROTOR SHAFT
SUPPORT ARMS

WORKING BLADES
(HYDROFOILS)

BEARINGS

Figure 11.12   Tidal fence vertical axis turbines (courtesy of Blue Energy Canada)

turbine of 60 m diameter. They operate at a minimum tidal velocity of about 2 m/second. Since the tidal flow is relatively constant, underwater turbines are subject to much less buffeting than their wind counterparts. According to Peter Fraenkel, director of Marine Current Turbines that have installed a demonstration turbine off the coast of Devon, the best tidal stream sites could generate 10 MW per square kilometre (see Fig 11.13).

A demonstration MCT is operating off the north coast of Devon with another planned for Strangford Lough in Northern Ireland. However, the first major deployment of this technology is being considered for the tidal race off the Channel Island of Alderney (see Fig. 11.14).

A problem with tidal energy is that, whilst it is predictable, it produces large bursts of energy at regular intermittent intervals. (see Fig. 11.15). As output approaches gigawatt scale this raises potential problems for the Grid and even more so for the generator if peak output

Figure 11.13 Tidal stream turbines or tidal mills, serviced above water (courtesy of Marine Current Turbines (MCT))

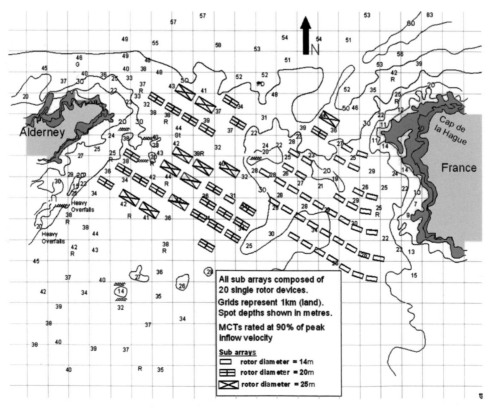

Figure 11.14 Suggested layout of underwater turbines off Alderney (courtesy of the Sustainable Energy Research Group, University of Southampton)

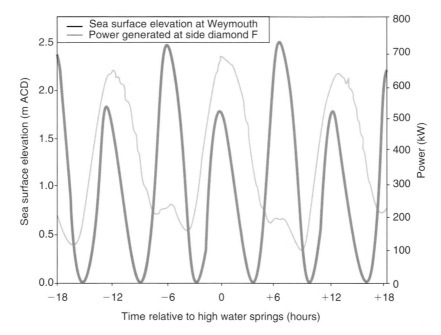

Figure 11.15   Power output of underwater turbines in the English Channel (courtesy of Southampton University)

coincides with the bottom of the market price. This is a problem experienced by Denmark when its domestic market has no demand for the excess wind power, and it has to export to Norway and Sweden in a buyers' market.

One answer is to use uneconomic power to release hydrogen by the electrolysis of water. This could then serve a fuel cell stack which could deliver energy at the peak of the price curve. This means that electricity could be delivered at around 45% efficiency which is better than the Grid. It does, however, not include the load factor of the turbines since this is, in effect, using surplus power which has a low to zero market value.

Alternatively the Redox Flow Battery is capable of storing multi-megawatt hours of electricity. It comprises very large twin cisterns containing electrolyte. One receives electricity under charge, the other discharges on demand. It is marketed, for example, by VRB Power Systems of Canada which is now developing a higher density system: the RGN flow battery. This technology could go some way to solving the problem of balancing power presented by intermittent renewables (see p. 131).

As fuel cells and electrolysers (which are reverse fuel cells) become more efficient and less expensive this strategy would be particularly appropriate for high-energy-density systems like the tidal energy bridge. It must also be remembered that fossil fuel prices are on a steady and probably irreversible upward trend as the 'peak oil' point is passed at ~2010.

Notes

1. Energy Paper No. 60, ETSU
2. Jackson T., 'Renewable Energy', summary paper for *Energy Policy*, Vol. 20, No. 9, pp. 861–863
3. *New Scientist*, 25 January 2003

12 Prospects for the energy infrastructure

The system of generating and distributing electricity is undergoing a slow but radical change. In political science there is a concept called the 'elitist perspective', which describes how individuals and groups assume control over social institutions. Elitist clusters exert power through the manipulation of individuals and governments to achieve their aims and maximize their profits. This is graphically illustrated by the $20 million given by US energy companies between 1999 and 2002 to politicians. Their reward was that 36 representatives from the energy industry were consulted by the Bush administration over future energy policy but no consumer or environmental groups were represented.[1] Worldwide energy companies share with pharmaceutical companies the pole position of influence over governments and continents. They will take concerted action when faced with a threat, as, for instance, by the phenomenon of global warming. Everything possible was done to undermine the credibility of the thousands of scientists who contributed to the three United Nations IPCC Scientific Reports on climate change.

Now, in the electricity supply and distribution sector their monopoly is being threatened by three major changes, which emerged during the end of the twentieth century. They have been defined by Carl J. Weinberg as follows:

- *Governance* – there has been a growing trend to admit competition and market-based approaches to the supply of energy. A consequence of this has been an erosion of central control in favour of diversified market-based enterprises. This has introduced consumers to the concept of choice in the buying of energy.
- *The environment* – there is growing support for the principle of sustainable development and an awareness of the environmental consequences of the unconstrained use of fossil fuels. The latter twentieth century saw an emphasis on the limitations of the carrying capacity of the Earth and the fact that, for the first time in history, a single species has changed the geophysical balance of the planet. The electricity supply industry will increasingly come under pressure as the major emitter of CO_2, the most abundant of human-induced greenhouse gases. Nature, it seems, has offered us a Faustian deal in the form of almost unlimited fossil-based energy for the next 100 years or more whilst ensuring that, if we take the deal, we will devastate the planet.
- Technology – there has been rapid progress in the development of renewable technologies and the emergence of smaller, modular, flexible technologies tailored to the needs of

individual consumers and managed by information technology which threatens the hegemony of the big power utilities.

Again, according to Weinberg, 'the conceptual model of a utility as large central power plants connected to [its] customers by wires may well not be the model for the future. This is particularly true for developing countries'.[2]

It is inherently difficult for big organizations with their bureaucratic hierarchies, their investment in plant and a large workforce tied in to a particular technology to adapt to radical change demanded by so-called 'disruptive technologies' like renewables. Furthermore, what is the incentive if they are still making substantial profits? Studies of technical innovation have revealed that radical innovations have never been introduced by market leaders.[3]

The state of California offers an example of how the market can rebel against the power of the utilities in response to increased gas prices, spiralling electricity costs – up to 40–50 cents per kWh – and insecurity of supply. Renewables suppliers offered a price of 8.5 cents per kWh fixed for three years. In other states wind energy electricity producers have offered 10–15 year contracts at 3–4 cents per kWh. Such low prices coupled with protection from the volatility of the utilities market are proving a most effective stimulus in attracting people to the renewables option.

In parallel with the awakening of this new concept of energy supply in the USA there has been a marked shift away from large, centralized generating plants to smaller, more localized units. In the 1970s the average output of power stations reached 150 MW, resulting from new large-scale nuclear and coal technology. With the decline of nuclear and the advent of independent power producers the average fell to 29 MW in the first half of the 1990s. So, already the energy infrastructure is moving in the direction of distributed and differentiated supply, which should flag a warning to governments that are planning large nuclear power plants for the future. They will be pushing against the tide.

Increasingly, power plants are being manufactured in assembly lines rather than constructed on site. They are available for small- and medium-size businesses and domestic users. The ultimate shift will come when fuel cells become economic and hydrogen readily available. The market is being stimulated, not just by green imperatives, but also by concerns about reliability and quality. The steady movement away from a 'resources' economy to a 'knowledge' economy is at the heart of this demand for quality and reliability. This embraces both the information-dependent enterprises like the financial markets and production-centred industries which rely on microprocessors. The Americans call this the 7/9s problem, i.e. 99% plus five nines. The grid can only provide 4/9s reliability, which translated means 99.99% reliability. This may seem adequate, but can result in significant losses due to down time. For example, for credit card operators it can amount to $2,580,000 per hour and for stockbrokers $6,480,000 per hour. In these circumstances minutes count yet the total adds up to about eight hours per year. What these operations require is 7/9s or 99.99999% reliability. When electricity storage facilities like advanced batteries and flywheels match small-scale production technologies, we can expect the distributed alternative to invade the electricity production market.

This, of course, will be emphatically opposed by the large utilities who will see their revenue streams threatened. One of their weapons is in setting interconnection requirements which fall under two headings: technical standards and administration. The technical standards relate to ensuring compatibility and quality before a supplier can be linked to the grid. At present the tendency is for the burden of proof that a proposed connection to the grid will not harm the system rests with the supplier not the utility. It is raising the issue that there must be national standards if distributed generation is to have an impact on the future. The same goes for administrative issues concerning how a system is to be inspected and certified, and, above all, the rate at which an independent generator is paid.

In the USA, 32 states have instituted 'net metering', which involves a small independent supplier having a meter capable of going into reverse so that the utility buys back power at the same price it sells to consumers. This is a facility urgently needed in the UK to stimulate the renewables market.

The ultimate configuration of energy supply may be the formation of numerous minigrids, enabling a much more precise matching of supply with demand within a local area. There may be various interconnections between minigrids and with the National Grid. Drawing from the National Grid would be regulated by specified conditions such as using the grid only for baseload requirements. Information technology is now capable of managing the complexities of a system with a large number of distributed resources without centralized control. It can deal with the interplay of supply and demand providing hour-by-hour least-cost outcomes to the benefit of consumers.

In the UK this fundamental reconfiguring of the energy supply system has been endorsed by the Royal Commission on Environmental Pollution which recommends:

> a shift from very large all electricity plant towards more numerous combined heat and power plants. The electricity system will have to undergo major changes to cope with this development and with the expansion of smaller scale, intermittent renewable energy sources. The transition towards a low-emission energy system would be greatly helped by the development of new means of storing energy on a large scale.[4]

The Washington Worldwatch Institute has also endorsed this scenario, stating that 'an electricity grid with many small generators is inherently more stable than a grid serviced by only a few large plants'. That was before 11 September 2001 and the terrorist demolition of the World Trade Center. Now the security of such plants has become a major issue. A dispersed system with many thousands of suppliers is immune to catastrophic failure.

It is unfortunate that many governments still consider renewables to be a sideshow in the scenarios for the energy future. Fossil fuels and nuclear power are still perceived as the dominant players for the next half century, which means a commitment to a centralized grid system operated by a small number of large utilities. Numerous factors are now making small-scale renewable generation attractive and this trend will escalate as the technologies improve and pressures to reduce CO_2 emissions increase as evidence of climate changes mounts. It would be the height of folly to commit to a system for decades to come which is highly vulnerable and which is already being supplanted by a wide range of renewable technologies which, for countries like the UK, could meet all energy needs, provided there is an energetic campaign to reduce demand. Because ultimately 'an electron saved is the cleanest option'.[5]

Towards a hydrogen economy

Over the millennia there have been three ages of energy. First there was the epoch of wood burning, lasting up to the eighteenth century when it was gradually supplanted by coal. The early twentieth century saw a gradual shift from coal to oil. The fourth energy age is dawning and will focus on hydrogen. Its drivers will be concern about security of supply of fossil fuels, anxieties about the environment especially global warming and, finally, advances in technology.

The concept of a hydrogen economy emerged from a group of General Motors engineers in the 1970s. However, at that time there was little incentive to switch from hydrocarbon fuels. Now things are different for a range of reasons.

The year 2001 marked the point at which the Gulf States controlled over 35% of world oil production. The significance of this figure is that it is said to be at a level at which a cartel of producers can control world oil prices. In the 1970s the world experienced two oil shocks engineered by the oil producers. The UK government has been warned that another similar oil shock could trigger a stock market collapse or even war. Since the September 11 outrage, that possibility has loomed larger.

All this makes hydrogen the most attractive option as the energy carrier for the future. Used for powering a fuel cell, its only by-products are heat and water. Even the Executive Director of GM Cars has conceded that 'our long-term vision is of a hydrogen economy'. To reinforce this his company, together with Ford, Daimler-Chrysler, Honda and Toyota, competed to be the first to market a fuel cell car by 2004. Time has proved this timescale to be optimistic. More realistic is the statement by a Vice President of Daimler-Chrysler, Professor Herbert Kohler, that for the next 20 years there will be a 'wider use of hybrids…After that, by about 2025, fuel cell technology will be widely available at competitive prices'. The President of Texaco Technology Ventures informed a US Scientific Committee of the House of Representatives that: 'Market forces, greenery and innovation are shaping the future of our industry and propelling us inexorably towards hydrogen energy'.

The viability of a hydrogen economy is also linked inexorably to the fortunes of the fuel cell. This is why enormous research resources are directed towards reducing the unit cost and raising the efficiency of all types of fuel cell.

The road ahead

There are two approaches to the adoption of hydrogen as the prime energy carrier of the future. The first is to extract hydrogen from a readily available fuel like natural gas or petrol. As stated earlier, this is done by a reformer unit. The sage of the green movement, Amory Lovins, claims that a reformer the size of a water heater 'can produce enough hydrogen to serve the fuel cells in dozens of cars'. The great advantage of this approach is that there already exists the infrastructure for natural gas which has the highest hydrogen content of all the candidates for reforming hydrogen. This could equally apply to buildings, with an individual house accommodating a reformer/fuel cell package which would supply both heat and power. In future, garages could reform natural gas on site to make it available at the pump. The downside is that readily accessible gas reserves are diminishing and the UK faces the prospect of buying 90% of its gas from nations on whom it would prefer not to be reliant.

Another problem is that, if there is a substantial investment in a national system involving the reforming of natural gas, there is the danger that this will 'lock-out' the direct use of hydrogen produced by electrolysis. From a renewable energy and environmental point of view the technological 'lock-in' of an inferior technology would be most regrettable.

An infrastructure carrying hydrogen produced directly from electrolysis is the second option. This poses the 'chicken and egg' problem. Manufacturers will not invest heavily in the development of fuel cells until there is the network of pipes to serve a critical mass of consumers. On the other hand, infrastructure providers will be loath to develop a network until fuel cells are cost-effective and have a strong foothold in the market.

Some experts claim that the incremental path to the hydrogen economy is the only realistic approach, arguing that a complete hydrogen infrastructure built from scratch would be prohibitively expensive. This argument is attractive to governments who would be expected to bear some of the capital costs of the enterprise. Others disagree, claiming that converting a natural gas network would not be 'prohibitively expensive' and that there would be economic and environmental costs associated with adopting a compromise solution with its lock-in risks.

As a distributed energy system matures, and PV and fuel cell efficiencies improve, so also will the opportunity for operators of domestic-size renewable installations to direct their electricity to a neighbourhood electrolyser unit with reformer backup to produce hydrogen to feed a community fuel cell which would, in turn, provide the cluster of homes with heat and power.

Such dedicated PV/hydrogen installations already exist. One example is in operation in Neunburg vorm Wald, Germany.

Solar energy offers one of the most abundant sources of electrolysed hydrogen. Deserts flanking the Mediterranean have already been mentioned as the ideal location for parabolic trough or parabolic dish reflectors to produce high-pressure steam to power steam turbines or Stirling engines to create the power to split water. The export of PV and solar hydrogen could transform the economies of some developing countries.

Hydrogen storage

This is the final hurdle for the hydrogen economy to negotiate before it reaches the final straight. Fuel cells depend on a steady supply of hydrogen, which means that storage backup is an essential component of the system where reformation is not involved.

The conventional storage method for hydrogen is pressurized tanks. The pressure varies according to volume: up to 50 litres requires 200–250 bar; larger amounts, 500–600 bar. Some very large containers can be as low as 16 bar.

It can be stored as a liquid but this necessitates cooling to −253°C and requires a heavily insulated tank.

Bonded hydrogen is another option. Granular metal hydrides store hydrogen by bonding it chemically to the surface of the material. The metal particles are charged by being heated and then receiving the hydrogen at high pressure. Some metals can absorb up to one thousand times their volume of hydrogen. On cooling, the hydrogen is locked into the metal and released by heating. The heat may come from a high-temperature fuel cell. For storage in buildings the most appropriate metal hydride is probably iron-titanium. It is too heavy for vehicle application but ideal for buildings having a relatively low operating temperature.

Recently, interest has been aroused by a storage technology which has emerged from Japan and Hong Kong. It consists of nanotubes of carbon, that is, sheets of carbon rolled into minute tubes 0.4 nm (0.4 billionths of a metre) in diameter. This is just the size to accommodate hydrogen atoms. A pack of carbon nanotubes has the potential to store up to 70% of hydrogen by weight compared to 2–4% of metal hydrides. Research is progressing into nanofibre graphite which could be a winner provided the team at Northeastern University in Boston can surmount its predilection for water over hydrogen.

A more exotic possibility was reported in *Scientific American* in May 2000. It referred to the capacity of solid molecular hydrogen to turn to metal at a pressure of 400–620 gigapascals (4–6 million atmospheres). Solid metallic hydrogen can store huge amounts of energy which is released as it returns to the gas phase.

If, as seems likely, the global warming curve is steeper than the official projections, then the pressure to switch to a hydrogen economy will become irresistible. Fortune will favour those countries who have developed a strong manufacturing base for a range of renewables which will be in heavy demand, not least in the developing countries. The problem of the 2 billion of the world's population who do not have access to electricity can only be solved by renewables and a distributed supply system.

The country which is on course to become the first hydrogen economy because it has a head start with its immense resources of geothermal and hydropower is Iceland. It plans to convert all cars, trucks, buses and boats to hydrogen over the next 30 years. It will also export hydrogen to Europe. Even more ambitious is the island of Vanuata in the Pacific Ocean. It is en route to achieve a 100% hydrogen economy by 2010 due to its abundance of renewable resources – geothermal, wind, solar and hydropower. Not to be outdone, Hawaii, which is rich in solar and geothermal resources (and, no doubt, wave), recently established a public–private partnership to promote hydrogen as a major player in the island's economy, even exporting the gas to California.

Electricity storage

A technology called 'regenesys' converts electrical energy to chemical energy and is potentially capable of storing massive amounts of electricity. Energy is stored in two concentrated aqueous electrolyte solutions, sodium bromide and sodium polysulphide. On charging the bromide ions are oxidized to bromine while sulphur in the polysulphide anions is converted to sulphide ions. On discharging, the sulphide ions act as the reducing agent and the tribromide ion as the oxidizing agent. The system can be switched from fully charging to discharging in about 20 milliseconds. The city of Toronto is investigating the feasibility of using the advance RGN flow battery as back-up for its grid during periods of peak demand to prevent outages and 'brown-outs' on such occasions. An appropriate 600 MWh urban scale storage system would need 30 million litres of electrolyte stored in 6 m high tanks covering the area of a football pitch. It is still considered more cost-effective than providing the extra generating capacity to meet the same demand.

In the opinion of the Royal Commission on Environmental Pollution, hydrogen and regenerative fuel cells will be in widespread operation by the middle of the century. If global warming and security of energy supply issues simultaneously become critical then viable large scale storage technologies will arrive much sooner.

Combined heat and power (CHP)

From time to time reference has been made in the text to CHP. Since there seems to be strong EU and UK government support for this system of energy distribution it calls for special consideration.

First, electricity generation in the UK is the largest single contributor to CO_2 emissions, amounting to 26% of the total. Many buildings are responsible for more CO_2 from the electricity they use than from the fuel for the boilers providing hot water and space heating. At the same time the heat from power stations is ejected to cooling towers and thence to rivers and the sea. The River Trent in the UK is almost suitable for tropical fish.

Combined heat and power can be scaled to meet almost any level of demand from a single home to a whole city. Already some cities like Sheffield receive heat and power from the incineration of municipal waste. However, this is not an ideal heat and power source for the future on account of its emissions. Importantly the infrastructure exists to be converted in the future to more environmentally benign producers of heat and power.

The European Commission aims to double the use of CHP by 2010. The UK government has a target of 10 GWe of CHP with associated carbon savings of six million tonnes per year, which represents 25% of its declared target savings or 20% by 2010.

A basic division in providing CHP is between factory-produced units up to 1 MWe and custom-built site-specific plants producing up to hundreds of megawatts. Rapid developments in the technology of small gas turbines and gas engines is helping to create favourable conditions for CHP which have an efficiency exceeding 70%. According to

David Green, Director of the CHP Association, a typical payback time for CHP is three to five years with an operating life of 15–20 years.

As stated earlier there is already an alpha-type Stirling engine on the market in the UK known as WhisperGen, producing 5 kW as heat and 800 W of electricity. On the verge of being market-ready is a 1 kWe, 15 kWth home CHP package based on a 'free-piston' Stirling engine under the name 'Microgen' (pp. 104 and 106).

In Chapter 9 there was reference to a domestic CHP package centred on a 1 kWe solid oxide fuel cell that can operate with natural gas. Ceres Power plans to market the system in 2007.

Community CHP systems using turbines powered by natural gas or, preferably, biogas from anaerobic digestion plants are a viable system now and could take off with the right government support. Housing estates now being built throughout the UK should be provided at the outset with an insulated hot water pipe infrastructure even though the system may not be operational initially. It is much more cost-effective to use a common trench at the construction stage than retrofit when the external works are complete.

The ultimate opportunity is for city-wide CHP. A genuine commitment to a sustainable future would require a government to promote and subsidise city-wide CHP using large, low-temperature water grids as used successfully in Denmark.

One option being proposed is to exploit the waste heat from large coal/oil fired or nuclear power stations. Nuclear power is enormously wasteful of heat, producing much more excess heat per unit of power than conventional power stations. Plants of this size are usually some distance from conurbations. However, Denmark again provides the prototype with the city of Aarhus receiving heat from a coal-fired plant 30 km distant. The rate of flow is around 3 m/second through large-diameter pipes.

However, with pressure increasing for the electricity infrastructure to evolve into a much more fragmented, distributed system, this would not be a wise investment. The capital commitment would inhibit conversion to a fundamentally different distribution system. This would be especially alarming in the case of nuclear power since it would establish a cost-effective argument (however flawed) for replacing the ageing nuclear plants with a new generation of nuclear power stations. The route ahead is for near zero carbon CHP plants fuelled by wood from rapid rotation crops or biogas from farm and municipal waste and the anaerobic conversion of sewage The ultimate CHP technology at city scale must be high-temperature fuel cells fed with direct piped hydrogen, but that is decades in the future.

CHP has advantages when used in conjunction with solar energy and wind power. Large plants between 100 and 300 MW of electrical capacity are flexible, having the ability to change their mode of operation from producing electricity alone to delivering both electricity and heat in varying proportions. This means that it can adjust its mode according to how much electricity is being provided from renewable sources. CHP is reliably available at times of system peak, being immune to the vagaries of wind or sun. It is therefore ideal for complementing renewable technologies.

There is a final twist to CHP. It can also provide cooling in so-called 'trigeneration' mode. Most trigeneration schemes are to be found in cities in the USA where air conditioning accounts for considerable electricity consumption. Piped chilled water can significantly reduce the electricity demand from air conditioning plants in large office complexes. Even a number of financial institutions in the City of London enjoy this facility.

Barriers to progress

A drawback which affects most renewables is the new electricity trading arrangement (NETA). This requires a provider of electricity to the National Grid to estimate in advance how much electricity they will be exporting. Suppliers who may be subject to quite large fluctuations in output due to the inconsistency of wind or sun are severely disadvantaged by this regulation.

Secondly, the UK conforms with the European Union in the way heat and power from CHP are evaluated. It is the heat which has prime value; the electricity is treated as a waste product which is a mechanism which Alice would recognize from Wonderland. It is like saying that the heat from a car radiator is of prime value and the distance travelled a worthless by-product.

It is essential that there is now consistency between the words of politicians in backing CHP and their actions in facilitating its widespread adoption. For a start, electricity from CHP must be ascribed its full value and that the contribution of embedded generation generally is fully acknowledged in legislation and in the returns which it offers to suppliers.

Conclusion

Whilst the UK expresses its commitment to the principle of distributed generation with contributions from thousands – perhaps millions – of contributors, in reality the dice is heavily loaded against small-scale generation and CHP. For example:

- There is a complex and lengthy process to be undertaken before a small contributor can be accepted by a distribution network operator (DNO).
- All the costs of providing the hardware for connection are borne by the small contributor.
- The UK government will not acknowledge what the real market situation is *vis a vis* renewables as against fossil fuels. First, renewables must be compensated for the avoided costs of pollution. Second, fossil fuels must have their subsidies removed. According to the Organization for Economic Co-operation and Development (OECD) 2002 report we are subsidising fossil-based energy to the tune of $57 billion per year. The report states: 'Through the provision of subsidies on fossil fuels, governments are effectively subsidising pollution and global warming as more than 60% of all subsidies flow to oil, coal and gas.' The playing field is going to take a lot of levelling.

The subsidy system in the UK has now largely been transferred to the Carbon Trust with an overall reduction in budget. The case of Germany makes an interesting comparison. It introduced a system of subsidies aiming to equip 100,000 roofs with PVs by 2003. To achieve this there are low interest loans (1.9% in 2001) and a bonus on the buy-back price. In 1999 the federal government introduced the Law for the Priority of Renewable Energy (REL). It came into operation in April 2000 with a buy-back price of 0.51 euros (c. 30p or US 45c) per kWh. The aim was to achieve installed power of 300 MWp by 2003. The effect had been dramatic and the target exceeded. For example, in Bavaria the installed PV capacity in 1999 was 2350 kW. In 2001 it had become 21,730 kW. A New Renewable Energy Law has since been enacted with a further 100,000 roofs target. The feed-in tariff is about 35p per kWh for small operators. The difference with the original law is that large-capacity generators now receive a subsidy which makes commercial scale operations a viable proposition. PV 'farms' up to 18 MW capacity have been installed as a result.

The stark truth is that small-scale renewables and distributed generation will never take off in the UK whilst they have to compete with the depressed and subsidised prices of fossil fuels. There are gestures in the right direction with Distribution Network Operators (DNOs) being required to take a percentage of their energy from major renewables sources like wind or biomass. However, the only way that the situation could be rectified in favour of small-scale renewables is for the example of Germany to be followed or for there to be a

Europe-wide carbon tax which recognizes the external costs and subsidies associated with fossil fuels.

Notes

1. *The Guardian*, 27 March 2002
2. op cit., p.37
3. Christensen, Clayton M. (1997), *The Innovators Dilemma: When New Technologies Cause Great Firms to Fall*, Harvard Business School Press
4. Twenty-second report, *Energy, The Changing Climate*, p.169, Stationery Office, London, 2000
5. Seth Dunn, *Renewable Energy World*, July/August 2001

13 Materials

Concrete

As possibly the most extensively used building material, concrete attracts criticism from environmentalists on account of its carbon-intensive production techniques and its use of a once-only natural resource, limestone. Cement is formed by heating clay and lime in a rotary kiln to a temperature of about 1450°C which produces some 3000 kg per tonne of CO_2. In addition, the heating process produces a chemical reaction through the conversion of calcium carbonate into calcium oxide which releases about 2200 kg of CO_2. Add to this the carbon miles in transportation, the impacts caused by mining etc., and concrete gains few points on the sustainability scale.

The UK Climate Change Levy is providing a powerful incentive for manufacturers to reduce CO_2 emissions since an 80% abatement of the tax can be granted in return for specific CO_2 abatement strategies. One method of reducing concrete's carbon impact is to use pulverized fuel ash (PVA) to reduce the proportion of cement in the concrete mix. These new blended cements contain up to 30% of PVA, a by-product of coal-fired electricity generation. This use of PVA has the further advantage of avoiding landfill costs whilst also reducing the need to quarry natural aggregates such as gravel. However, it must be remembered that it is the waste product of carbon-intensive coal-fired power stations. It also contains some toxic chemicals. Its availability will decline as coal-fired power stations are phased out.

The mountains of slate waste which encircle Blaenau Ffestioniog in north Wales are destined to become a powdered aggregate in the near future. This will offer the double benefit of avoiding depleting a natural resource and also drastically improving the amenity value of an area scarred by slate mining over the centuries.

The development of the technology of geopolymers offers the prospect of a more eco-friendly concrete. Geopolymerization is a geosynthesis which is a reaction that chemically bonds minerals to form molecules that are structurally comparable to the molecules which provide the strength to rocks. In the opinion of Jean Davidovits of the French Geopolymer Institute at St Quentin, these 'geopolymeric' concretes would reduce CO_2 emissions associated with conventional concrete by 80–90%. This is said to be due to the avoidance of calcination from calcium carbonate and the lower kiln temperature of 750°C. The market availability of this material is said to be at least five years away.[1]

Recycled crushed concrete has been used for some time for low-grade applications like road construction. It is now being heralded as being suitable for less demanding structural elements. One attraction of this material is that it gains a BREEAM (Building Research Establishment Environmental Assessment Method) credit if used in sufficient quantity. The main disadvantage of the material concerns quality control. A consignment may contain concrete from numerous sites, which means that each batch must be tested by being sieved and chemically analysed to check its ingredients and quality.[2,3]

Glass

The RIBA conference that initiated this book included the introduction by Pilkington Architectural of their Triple Planar glass. This is a glazing system that eliminates the need for framing, with the junction between panes sealed with 10–12 mm of silicon. The importance of this system is that it can achieve a U-value of $0.8\,W/m^2K$, which should make it highly attractive for commercial application when coupled with its aesthetic appeal.[4]

A wider market can be expected for Pilkington's electrochromic glass, marketed as Econtrol. This works by passing a low electrical voltage across a microscopically thin coating to the glass, activating a tungsten-bearing electrochromic layer which can darken in stages. Electricity is only used to change the state of the coating, not to sustain its level of transmittance. About 3 volts are needed to effect the change, and this could be provided by the building energy management system or be individually controlled by occupants, allowing for fine-tuning to immediate needs. PV cells integrated into a façade or roof could easily supply this level of power.

This system offers several advantages. Foremost is the fact that it can save energy. It avoids overheating and solar glare. Trials conducted in Germany indicated that it can save up to 50% of the energy required for air conditioning. Even when the glass is fully darkened, external views are maintained. The avoided cost of external shading must also be factored into the cost-benefit analysis.

The first building to feature Econtrol was a bank in Dresden. The electrochromic glazing on the southern elevation is over 17 m high and 8 m wide. The glass can be switched to give five levels of light and heat transmittance.

Finally, in 2002, Pilkington introduced 'hydrophilic' glass to the market. This is a self-cleaning glass which goes under the name of Pilkington Activ. Layers are deposited on the glass during the float manufacturing process to produce the photocatalytic characteristics of the glass. After exposure to ultraviolet (UV) light in daylight, the coating reacts chemically in two ways. First it breaks down organic deposits – tree sap, bird droppings etc. – by introducing extra molecules of oxygen into the deposit. This has the effect of accelerating the rate of decay. Second, the coating causes the glass to become hydrophilic. This means that droplets of rain coalesce to form sheets of water which slide down the glass, removing dirt particles in the process. The really smart aspect of the product is that the coating stores enough UV energy during the day to sustain the process overnight.

The avoidance of cleaning costs, especially for commercial buildings, could offer considerable annual savings, especially where atria are concerned. For householders it could, in the long term, spell the end of the local friendly window cleaner.

Now that nanotechnology has taken a hold on glass manufacturers, all kinds of possibilities can be envisaged; for example, glass that responds instantly to changes in weather or that is an integrated photovoltaic electricity generator.

Insulation

There is an increasing demand for eco-insulation materials that are obtained from natural sources. The most popular up to the present is cellulose fibre derived from recycled newspaper.

The material is treated with boron to give fire resistance and protect against vermin infestation. It is suitable for wet spray or dry blown application. One of the most popular proprietary brands is 'Warmcell', supplied by Excel Industries which belongs to Fillcrete. It has a thermal conductivity of 0.036 W/mK, which puts it in the same category as most of the main insulants on the market. It has BBA (British Board of Agreement) certification. Warmcell is an integral part of Fillcrete's 'breathing wall' panel system suitable for structural walls, floor and roof components. The panels have a U-value of 0.19 W/m^{2}K. The panels incorporate service ducts on the internal face to facilitate rapid on-site fixture of services.

Prefabrication is becoming increasingly popular. This is because elements are produced in controlled conditions and safe from the elements. Because of their extremely tight tolerances they can offer guaranteed air tightness, which is a prerequisite for highly energy efficient buildings.

Other manufacturers of cellulose fibre insulation include Construction Resources supplying Isofloc, and 'Save It' (Nottingham) producing Ecofibre. These also are BBA certified.

Coming more into prominence is sheep's wool. One of the first buildings to use wool as an insulant was the exhibition House of the Future within the Museum of Welsh Life in south Wales. It uses 200 mm of wool in its cavities. At the time it had to be imported from France. Now the UK has its own treatment facilities and it can be obtained from the Wool Marketing Board. It has to be treated with water-based boron.

The most ambitious use of sheep's wool for insulation in the UK is in what is claimed to be the largest commercial ecobuilding in the UK, erected by the Centre for Alternative Technology (CAT) at Machynlleth in Wales. The installed thickness is 325 mm and the wool was hand-sprayed with boron during installation.

A demonstration project in Scotland is currently being evaluated to test the effectiveness of hemp as an insulation material. The verdict so far is that the hemp homes are using significantly less energy than was predicted by the SAP ratings and U-value calculations. They are consistently outperforming the control houses which have conventional masonry construction with cavity insulation. This is a material to watch.

Natural Building Technologies of High Wycombe was established to promote the widespread use of natural building products. These include cellulose fibre, cork and sheep's wool. All these natural materials are hygroscopic, that is, they absorb moisture without any damage to their functional integrity. Water vapour can move through them, which makes them ideal for 'breathing' walls which offer short-term protection against condensation. The big benefit is in offsetting the need for vapour barriers, which are notorious for being at the mercy of operatives on site.

The emergence of transparent insulation materials (TIMs) offers the double benefit of providing insulation and space heating. One product, StoTherm Solar, consists of a honeycomb structure of glass-coated polycarbonate. It is produced by the external insulation specialists Sto AG. It is claimed that a southerly façade using StoTherm Solar could achieve an energy gain of 120 kWh/m^2 per year. In winter the outside temperature might be as low as $-10°$C. Despite this, the back of the TIM could be as high as 60°C, benefiting from the low angle of the sun. Since the TIM is bonded to the inner wall surface this warmth would be transmitted to the interior, producing a room temperature of around 20°C. That is on the assumption that the wall is of solid construction with a density of at least 1200 kg/m^3. Even on north-facing elevations this technology could offer an energy gain of up to 40 kWh/m^2 per year.

Saving energy is one thing; buildings as carbon sinks is another, yet this is the destiny of buildings according to John Harrison, a technologist from Hobart, Tasmania. He has produced a magnesium-carbonate-based 'ecocement'. In the first place it only uses half the energy for process heating required by calcium carbonate (Portland) cement. The roasting process produces CO_2 but most of this is reabsorbed by a process of carbonation as the cement hardens. Using ecocement for such items as concrete blocks means that nearly all the material will eventually carbonate, resulting in an absorption rate of 0.4 tonnes of CO_2 for every tonne of concrete. The ultimate ecocredential of this material is the rate of carbon sequestration. According to Harrison, 'The opportunities to use carbonation processes to sequester carbon from the air are just huge. It can take conventional cements centuries or even millennia to absorb as much as ecocements can absorb in months'.[5] This means that an ecoconcrete tower block can perform the same function as growing trees as it steadily fixes carbon. Harrison estimates that a shift to ecocement could ultimately cut CO_2 emissions by over one billion tonnes since it could replace 80% of uses currently served by Portland cement.

There is one further attribute to this material. Being less alkaline than Portland cement it can incorporate up to four times more waste in the mix than conventional cement to provide bulk without losing strength. This could include organic waste which would otherwise be burnt or added to landfill, sawdust, plastics, rubber and fly ash.

Ecocement is not unique in its pollution-absorbing properties. Mitsubishi is producing paving slabs coated with titanium dioxide which remove most pollutants from the air. In Japan 50 towns are already using them and in Hong Kong it is estimated that they remove up to 90% of the nitrogen oxides that create smog. Magnesium-based concrete coated with titanium dioxide could be the basis for ecocities of the future.

Smart materials

Already a smart material has figured here, namely electrochromic glass.

According to Philip Ball, Associate Editor for Physical Sciences with the Journal *Nature*:

> *Smart materials represent the epitome of the new paradigm of materials science whereby structural materials are being superseded by functional ones. Smart materials carry out their tasks as a result of their intrinsic properties. In many situations they will replace mechanical operations. We will see smart devices in which the materials themselves do the job of levers, gears and even electronic circuitry. There is even the prospect of a house built of bricks that change their thermal insulating properties depending on the outside temperature so as to maximize energy efficiency.[6]*

Materials like thermochromic glass (which darkens in response to heat) come into the general category of *passive* smart materials. The really exciting advances are in *active* smart materials. An active system is controlled not only by external forces but also by some internal signal. In smart systems an active response usually involves a feedback loop that enables the system to 'tune' its response and thus adapt to a changing environment rather than be passively driven by external forces. An example is a vibrating-damping smart system. Mechanical movement triggers a feedback loop into providing movement that stabilizes the system. As the frequency or amplitude of the vibrations change so the feedback loop modifies the reaction to compensate.

One useful class of smart materials are 'shape memory alloys' (SMAs), alternatively called 'solid state phase transformations'. These are materials which, after deformation, return completely to their former shape. They function by virtue of the fact that the crystal structures of SMAs change when heated. An application already being exploited is as thermostats, where bimetal strips are replaced by alloys. They can be incorporated into mechanisms for operating ventilation louvres or ventilation/heating diffusers.

In general smart systems can be divided into sensors and actuators. Sensors are detection devices which respond to changes in the environment and warn accordingly. Actuators make things happen; they are control devices that close or open an electrical circuit or close or open a pipe. In fact they can be tailored to serve both functions. For example, they may perform a dual role, extracting heat from low-grade sources like groundwater or geothermal reservoirs and serve as mechanical pumps to deliver the warmed water to the heating system of a building. No moving parts; no possibility of mechanical breakdown and all at low cost; it seems 'such stuff as dreams are made of' and may well transform the prospects for such technologies as heat pumps.

In principle, SMAs can be used for any application which requires heat to be converted into mechanical action.

Smart fluids

By introducing a strong electrical field, certain fluids can change to a near solid state. They are called 'electrorheological fluids' (rheology is the study of the viscosity and flow capacity of fluids). They can be made intelligent by coupling them to sensor devices which detect sudden movement. They have the potential to replace a range of mechanical devices such as vehicle clutches, springs and damping devices to eliminate mechanical vibrations.

Another class of smart fluid is activated by being exposed to a magnetic field. Linked to sensors, they would be ideal for buildings in earthquake zones. Buildings would be constructed off concrete rafts which in turn would be supported by an array of magnetorheological dampers. At the onset of vibrations these would instantly change from solid to fluid and soak up the movement of the earth. In Tokyo and Osaka several recent buildings already exploit vibration damping and variable stiffness devices to counteract seismic movement.

There is yet another dimension to the characteristics of smart materials – materials that learn, that get smarter as they get older. They have an inbuilt degree of intelligence and are capable of optimizing their performance in response to feedback information.

What we will see in the near future are smart structures equipped with an array of fibre optic 'nerves' that will indicate what a structure is 'feeling' at any given moment and give instant information of any impending catastrophic failure. If the end of the last century was characterized by the rise of high technology with ever more complex electronic wizardry packed into ever smaller spaces, the future, according to materials scientists, 'may hold an increasing simplicity, as materials replace machines'.[7] We will learn to be adaptive rather than assertive. This surely is what environmental responsibility is all about.

Notes

1. www.geopolymer.org
2. www.bre.co.uk
3. For further information refer to *Ecotech 5*, in association with *Architecture Today*, 5 May 2002
4. www.pilkington.com/planar
5. 'Green Foundations', *New Scientist,* 13 July 02, p. 40
6. *Made to Measure*, Princeton, 1997, p. 104
7. Ball, op cit., p. 142

14   The photonic revolution

The end of the twentieth century witnessed a transformation in the power of light. It has already revolutionized communications and promises to do the same for illumination, in both cases resulting in substantial savings in energy.

The microelectronic transformation of the communications infrastructure which occurred over the last two decades is based on the capacity of semiconductors such as silicon to control electric currents. That control depends on a feature called the 'band gap' and it is the characteristics of that gap which determine which electrons are blocked from travelling through the semiconductor.

The light-emitting diode (LED)

Scientists have produced materials which have a photonic band gap, namely a range of wavelengths of light which are unable to pass through the material. This is achieved by structuring the materials in precisely designed patterns at the nanoscopic scale. The result has been called 'semiconductors of light'.

Light emitted from traditional forms of illumination is effectively a by-product of heat. The incandescent light bulb operates at 2000°C so clearly much of the energy it uses is wasted.

There is an alternative which leans heavily on quantum theory, which states that an atom's electrons emit energy whenever they jump from a high to a low energy level. Provided that the difference between the two levels is in the right range, the surplus energy is manifest as a flash of light – a photon. The wavelength and thus the colour of the light is determined by the size of the energy gap and this, in turn, depends on the atoms involved.

The principle behind the semiconductor light-emitting diode is that quantum transitions can take place within a solid. In an appropriate material some electrons are free to move whilst others are bound to the atoms. The difference between the energy state of these two types of electron is termed the 'band gap'. The application of a small electric current to a diode made from a semiconductor raises electrons to a higher energy state. As the electrons pass through the band gap they generate photons at a wavelength determined by the size of the gap. An appropriate semiconductor produces photons in the visible spectrum to create the LED.

Up to the present it has not been possible to make an LED that emits pure white light. To get close to this goal a combination of LEDs emitting red, green and blue light mixes these hues to produce a warm white light. The blue light has been a stumbling block but recently researchers in Japan made a chip using the semiconductor gallium nitride which emits blue light. This completed the triad of hues.

One of the criteria for judging the quality of artificial light is the degree to which it approximates to sunlight. This is measured by a colour rendering index (CRI) in which 100 represents absolute affinity. Incandescent bulbs have a score of 95 against the best LEDs, which achieve 85. However, it is at the level of efficiency that LEDs leave the rest of the field behind. Incandescent bulbs produce 10–20 lumens per watt whilst LEDs emit 100 lumens per watt. Furthermore, they have a life expectancy of about 50,000 hours. Their durability is measured in years, perhaps even decades.

However, there is a problem with the whitish light produced by mixing blue, red and green LEDs in that the human eye is not as sensitive to light at the blue and red ends of the visible spectrum as it is to the green. Consequently much of the power used to generate blue and red light is wasted. This problem has been addressed by Frederick Schubert of the Centre for Photonics Research at the University of Boston. In January 2000 it was reported that he had produced an LED which took into account the sensitivities of the human eye. The result was an LED emitting white light at the highest possible efficiency.

His answer was a device called a 'photon recycling semiconductor' (PRS-LED), which uses electrical power to generate photons at a single wavelength. Some of the photons are recycled to produce light at a different wavelength. The two wavelengths are calculated to produce the effect of white light. Schubert's device uses blue and orange to achieve this effect. The blue light is produced by an LED made of gallium, nitrogen and indium. The second semi-conductor layer consists of gallium, indium and phosphorus. The band gap of this second layer material has been adjusted to produce orange light. The claimed efficiency of this device is 330 lumens per watt (see Fig. 14.1).

This LED is still in the laboratory and the research effort is focused on improving its CRI and improving its efficiency so that a PRS-LED measuring less than a square centimetre will emit as much light as a 60 watt bulb whilst using only three watts of power. This highlights another virtue of this technology – its compactness. The absence of a glass bulb and bulky connections makes this a truly versatile form of illumination capable of being integrated into walls, ceilings and even floors. There are also moves to create LEDs which respond to changes in daylight level by adjusting their colour and brightness.

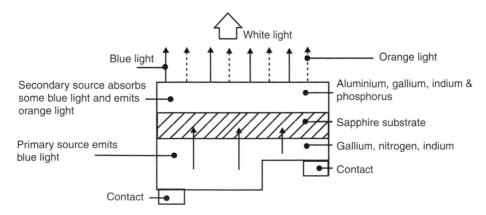

Figure 14.1   The Schubert Photon Recycling Semiconductor (PRS-LED) (derived from *New Scientist* article 'The end of light as we know it', 8 January 2000)

Even more radical is the suggestion by Ton Begemann of Eindhoven University that an LED lighting system might also be a carrier of information. He claims it would be possible to modulate the power supply to the LED in such a way as to enable it to carry digital information but at speeds too fast for the eye to detect. A pager, sensor or computer would be able to decode the message, making the light on the desk a node in a communication system via the electricity supply network.

The greatest benefit of all would be in the saving of energy. In most commercial buildings lighting is the main consumer of electricity. Colin Humphreys, a materials scientist at Cambridge University, estimates that LEDs would cut lighting bills by 80%. The reduction in carbon dioxide emissions due to lighting would also approach that percentage. Transposed to the scale of a nation, if all the light sources in the USA were converted to LEDs, this would cancel out the need for new power stations for 20 years, assuming the present rate of increase in electricity consumption of 2.7% per year.

As yet LEDs are not cost-effective set against conventional light sources. A Schubert 60 watt equivalent LED would cost $100. However, this is a technology which is bound to succeed, especially if the avoided cost of pollution and carbon dioxide emissions is factored into the cost-benefit analysis. Already 8% of US traffic signals use red LEDs. Developments in the technology coupled with economies of scale should enable LEDs to swamp the market within a decade. This will qualify them as one of the leading technologies in the fight to combat global warming.

Photonics in communication

Fibre optics are now a familiar feature of long-range communication. An optical fibre consists of a glass core and a cladding layer wrapping around it. The core and cladding are precisely chosen so that their refractive indices (the ability to bend light by specific amounts) ensure that the photons within the core are always reflected at the interface of the cladding (see Fig. 14.2).

This ensures that the only way light can escape is through the ends of the fibre. Either an LED or a laser sends electronic data that have been converted to photons along the fibre at a wavelength of between 1200 and 1600 nanometres. The most advanced fibres can send a light signal for about 50 miles without the need to boost the signal. Until the early 1990s the boosters were electronic, which created a bottleneck in the system. The answer was to insert stretches of fibre that were infused with ions of the rare earth element erbium. When the erbium-doped fibres are irradiated by a laser light the excited ions refresh the fading signal. This has resulted in dramatic improvements in capacity and speed – up to tens of gigabits per second. At the same time this refreshing facility can boost the power of many wavelengths simultaneously, so that it is now possible to send 160 frequencies in parallel and supply a total bandwidth of 400 gigabits per second over a fibre. Visible on the horizon is a fibre capacity of 300 to 400 terabits a second. New technology could break the petabit barrier (a petabit is ten to the power of fifteen bits). It will not come a moment too soon.

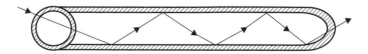

Figure 14.2 Optical fibre

In February 2000 the computer network at Kent State University in the USA came to a virtual standstill when thousands of hits from the music file-sharing utility Napster invaded emails from the Vice Chancellor and research data on genetic engineering. This gives credence to the nightmare scenario that a video-Napster capable of downloading anything from *Birth of a Nation* to *Rocky IV* could bring down the entire Internet.[1] On-line virtual reality could overwhelm the system with up to 10 petabits per second, which is 10,000 times greater than present-day traffic. Linked computers sharing power called metacomputing could require 200 petabit capacity.

The only transmission medium capable of meeting this challenge is a fibre optic system which is not inhibited by electronic switching. At present the problem is that the most advanced networks transmitting 10 billion bits per second threaten to choke the processing units and microchip memories in electronic switches. It's as though a ten-lane motorway suddenly contracts to a country lane. The gigabit tidal wave of photonic data has to be broken up into slower data streams that can be converted to electronic processing. Then the sequence has to be reversed to produce the fast flowing photonic mode. The answer is photonic switching, the holy grail of photonics research.

Eliminating the electronic stage of transmission has been the aim of Japanese scientists in Tsukuba. In May 2001 they claimed to have created an optical transistor that would pave the way for all-optical networks. Basically they have found a way to make one light beam make another disappear, thereby creating an optical semiconductor.

Huge amounts of venture capital are being directed at this developing field of science. In the first nine months of 2000 venture funding for optical networks totalled $3.4 billion. The attraction for this kind of investor is that the cost of transmitting a bit of optical information is halving every nine months.

Soon the whole world will be linked to an optical fibre superhighway based on photonic materials. One consequence is that teleworking will become much more prevalent, enabling commercial enterprises to scale down their centralized operations. High-capacity communication systems based on a multimedia super corridor accommodating audio, computer and visual communication will have a major impact on work patterns. Already teleconferencing is reducing the need for costly gatherings of executives as companies spread their operations globally. This will offer much greater freedom to employees as regards their place of abode.

The most recent development in IT is known as 'tele-immersion', described by *Scientific American* as 'a new telecommunications medium which combines virtual reality with video-conferencing. [It] aims to allow people separated by great distances to interact naturally as though they were in the same room' and 'involves monumental improvements in a host of computing technologies . . . Within ten years tele-immersion could be a substitute for many types of business travel'.[2] Photonic switching is perhaps the most monumental improvement that heralds a quantum change in the architecture of computers which are already approaching the barrier imposed by the physics of electronic processing. Not only will this next generation of computers have vastly increased capacity, they will achieve this with a fraction of the power consumed by present day machines. They will also avoid the heat gains of electronic processors. So the combination of LEDs and photonic computers will dramatically reduce the energy requirements of a typical office building, not only in terms of lighting and computing load but also in reducing the cooling load on the ventilation system.

A note of caution to conclude this chapter. One outcome of the exponential development of IT is that the economic and business certainties of the twentieth century are disintegrating. As electronic commerce grows, governments will find it ever harder to raise taxes. Each day trillions of dollars move around the global money market as corporations locate their transactions in low tax jurisdictions. Add to this the fact that people are increasingly obtaining goods and services via the Internet from places with the lowest taxes and it is clear that national governments will have diminishing power to raise revenue, with obvious consequences for the social services.

One scenario is that the growing gap between the poor and the affluent will continue to widen. The dividing line will become sharply defined as between those with IT and communication skills who can keep up with the pace of change and those who increasingly fall behind in this new Darwinian environment. As Ian Angell (head of the Department of Information Systems, London School of Economics) puts it:

> *People with computer skills are likely to end up winners. Those without are likely to emerge as losers. The power of the nation state will weaken. Communities that invest substantially in communication technologies will thrive. Those who don't, or those whose citizens are isolated from the new ways to communicate, will suffer. Change is inevitable. The Information Age will be kindest to those who adapt.*[3]

Notes

1.   *Scientific American*, January 2001
2.   *Scientific American*, April 2001, p. 54
3.   *New Scientist*, 4 March 2001, pp. 44–45

15   Building integrated renewable energy: case studies

Malmö – city of the future

The development on the waterfront of this southern city in Sweden was given its initial impetus by exhibition Bo01, masterminded by Professor Klas Tham and aimed at promoting sustainable urban development. The significance of this project is that it seeks to reconcile the goals of sustainable design with the demands of the market. Malmö is set to experience a renaissance in its fortunes with the completion of the Oresund Bridge linking it to Denmark. This project represents an emphatic statement of intent as the new gateway to Sweden.

The development occupies the Vastra Hamnen site formerly dedicated to industrial and dockside use. About 30 hectares is now occupied by a wide range of apartments by a selection of international architects including Ralph Erskine. The city laid down a number of conditions for the leases. The programme included statements about the overall character of the development including criteria for colours and ecological credibility of materials. An essential part of the development was the 'green space factor' providing parkland and foliage to compensate for the built-over area (see Fig. 15.1).

Building performance included the stipulation that energy use must be less than $105\,kWh/m^2/yr$. The overall plan aims to obtain 100% of the community's electricity from renewable sources such as a 2 MW wind turbine and $120\,m^2$ of PVs (see Fig. 15.2).

A heat pump drawing warmth from an underground aquifer and seawater is anticipated to meet 83% of district heating needs. The same system will provide cooling in summer. Of the remaining heat demand around 15% will be provided by $2000\,m^2$ of solar collectors and the rest from biogas derived from waste and sewerage. The energy is distributed by district heating/cooling mains.

Another prerequisite was that there should be a mix of social and luxury accommodation. The market-led pressures ensured that the expensive properties had the best outlooks with views over the sea or canal. This means that most of the apartments have east–west facing glazing – a case of outlook taking precedence over solar orientation.

An important component of the development is the inclusion of non-residential ground floor space for small businesses with access to the first floor to permit living above the premises.

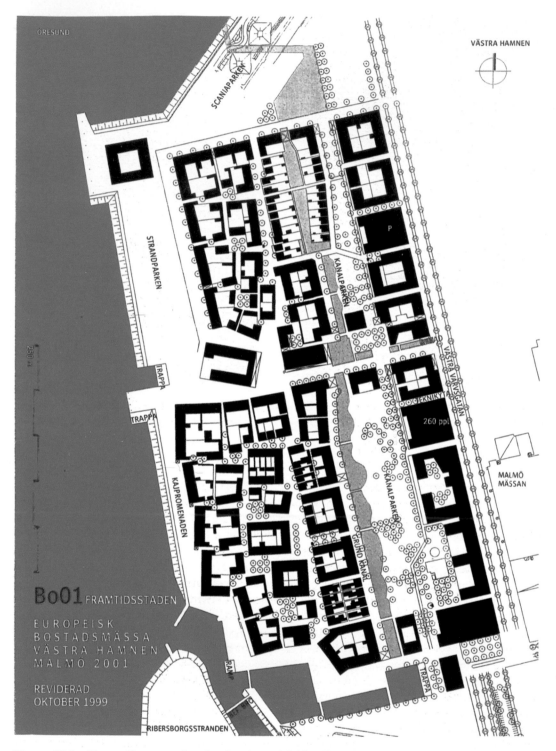

Figure 15.1   Vastra Hamnen site plan for the exhibition Bo01, 2001

Figure 15.2   Solar collectors operated by Sydcraft, a district energy supplier on the Tegelborden block on the Sundspromenaden (architect: Mansson Dahlback; photograph: Christopher John Hancock)

There is a highly disciplined transport policy for the site. Streets are car free and parking is limited to one space per dwelling. However, the real innovation is the provision of a pool of electric vehicles charged by wind power to enable the residents to reach the city centre. A neighbourhood garage provides natural gas/biogas for alternative fuel cars.

Surprisingly there is no facility for harvesting rainwater which is directed via the canal to the sea. Wastewater goes to the city's main treatment plant. However, there is a sophisticated system for the management of other kinds of waste which comprises an underground twin pipe vacuum tube collection network. Residents have access to twin terminals, one for food waste, the other for residual dry waste which is incinerated. Biogas and compost are obtained from the food waste. The city has constructed a reactor to convert organic waste into biogas and fertilizer. The biogas is returned to the apartments via the gas main. Nutrients and phosphorus are extracted from sewerage to be used as fertilizer with the residue used as fuel for the incinerator. It is estimated that reclaiming waste generates 290 kWh/yr of energy for every resident.

The final innovation is the fact that all households are connected to a broadband communication network which provides information on a wide range of topics. This includes the ability to monitor the use of energy and water and to exploit an environmental advice channel as well as such essential data as the time the next bus will arrive at the nearest bus stop.

The overall impact of Vastra Hamnen is of a project which has, with its variety of architects, achieved a reconciliation between market forces and environmental priorities.

Figure 15.3   Mount Cenis In-service Training Centre, Herne–Sodingen, Germany

The masterplan has maximized the contrast between the expansive views to the sea and intimate green spaces encompassed by the apartments. A further asset is the parkland adjacent to the canal which all adds up to an urban complex which capitalizes on the spectacular location of the site. The dialectic between public and private space, between hard and soft landscape, between introvert and extrovert space makes this a stimulating example of twenty-first century urban design. The final seal on the scheme will be the residential tower by Santiago Calatrava called the 'Turning Torso' which may sound more poetic in Swedish. It was completed in 2005. If there has to be a criticism it is that architectural individuality has priority over a consistent urban grain. But with an exhibition site that is to be expected. Altogether it is not a bad template for a 'city of the future'.

Government Training Centre, Germany

Possibly the most ambitious example of building-integrated PV (BIPV) to date is at the heart of the Ruhr in Germany at Herne–Sodingen. The Mount Cenis Government Training Centre, for a time the world's most powerful solar electric plant is a spectacular demonstration of the country's commitment to rehabilitate this former industrial region whilst also signalling the country's commitment to ecological development (see Fig. 15.3).

After the demise of heavy industry the Ruhr became a heavily polluted wasteland which prompted the government of North-Rhine Westphalia to embark on an extensive regeneration programme covering 800 square kilometres.

The building is, in effect, a giant canopy encompassing a variety of buildings and providing them with the climate of the Mediterranean. At 168 m long and 16 m high, the form and scale of the building has echoes of the huge manufacturing sheds of former times. A timber structural frame of rough-hewn pine columns is a kind of reincarnation of the forests from which they originated.

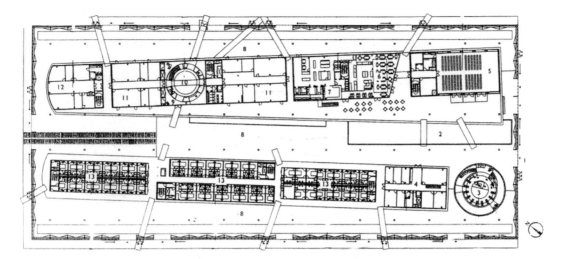

Figure 15.4   Mount Cenis ground floor plan

The structure encloses two three-storey buildings either side of an internal street running the length of the building (see Fig. 15.4).

The concrete structure provides substantial thermal mass, balancing out both diurnal and seasonal temperature fluctuations. Landscaped spaces provide social areas which can be used all year in a climate akin to the Cote d'Azur. Sections of the façade can be opened in summer to provide cross ventilation.

The building is designed to be self-sufficient in energy. The roof and façade incorporate 10,000 m² of PV cells integrated with glazed panels. Two types of solar module were employed: monocrystalline cells with a peak efficiency of 16% and lower-density polycrystalline cells at 12.5%. These provide a peak output of one megawatt. Six hundred converters change the current from DC to AC to make it compatible with the grid. A 1.2 MW battery plant stores power from the PVs, balancing output fluctuations. The power generated greatly exceeds the needs of the building at 750,000 kWh per year. German policy on renewables makes exporting to the grid a profitable proposition.

This is not the only source of energy generation. The former mines in the area release more than one million cubic metres of methane, which is used to provide both heat and power. Capturing the gas in this way results in a reduction of carbon dioxide emissions of 12,000 tonnes.

This complex is an outstanding example of an alliance between green technology and aesthetics. The architects, Jourda and Perraudin of Paris, designed the distribution of PV panels to reflect the arbitrary distribution of clouds by means of six different types of module with different densities, creating subtle variations to the play of light within the interior. It all adds up to an enchanting environment of spaciousness, light and shade. At the same time it affords a graphic reminder that regenerated industrial landscapes do not have to be populated by featureless utilitarian sheds.

National Trust Offices, Swindon, UK

A cutting edge office building in the UK is the National Trust offices in Swindon by architects Fielden Clegg Bradley. Despite being a 'design and build' contract, the nominated architects were able to deliver a state of the art sustainable building. It is naturally ventilated and daylit,

Figure 15.5   National Trust offices, Swindon (courtesy of Fielden Clegg Bradley)

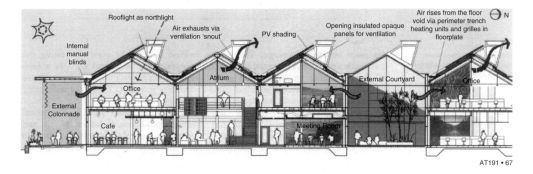

Figure 15.6   National Trust offices: ventilation and daylighting (courtesy of Fielden Clegg Bradley)

with mechanically assisted heat recovery ventilation for the winter. The majority of the roof supports PVs. Enhanced thermal insulation and lighting controls are featured and the whole building achieves an air tightness of $5.5\,m^3/m^2$. Many of its materials were sourced from the Trust's own sites. The architects had to work within the constraint that additional sustainability features had to pay back within 20 years. The building is on the site of an extensive nineteenth century railway works. The design echoes the scale and form of the old buildings whilst providing an office environment which should set the standard for offices of the future (see Figs 15.5 and 15.6). In 2006 it received the RIBA Sustainable Building of the Year award.

CIS Tower, Manchester, UK

It is still the case that most PV arrays on buildings are installed for reasons that do not include cost-effectiveness. However, that could change if the cost of the PVs is absorbed into the overall cost of a building refurbishment.

The façades of most commercial offices are of the curtain wall variety, which can be relatively easily dismantled. Re-façading presents an ideal opportunity for employing building-integrated renewable energy. Integrating PVs into a curtain wall can be a cost-effective solution when the avoided cost of a conventional solution is taken into account. This is what persuaded the Co-operative Insurance Society to refurbish the service element of the CIS Tower in Manchester with PVs. It is the first example in the UK of a really ambitious commercial PV installation as a retrofit strategy with an estimated output of 180,000 kWh/ year (see Fig. 15.7).

Figure 15.7   CIS Tower, Manchester with retro-fitted PVs (photograph: Pam Smith)

Eden Project Phase 4: Education Resource Centre – the Core

In the spring of 2006 the Core was completed (see Fig. 15.8). The design by Grimshaw Architects is heavy with symbolism such as its overall form based on the Ethiopian Tree of Knowledge where people would congregate to receive knowledge passed down from the elders. The spiral gridshell of the roof reflects the arrangement of florets at the centre of the sunflower which conforms to 'Fibonacci phylotaxis'. The Fibonacci series popularized in the thirteenth century is a sequence where each successive number is the product of the two previous numbers. It is linked with aesthetics in that the ratio between any two numbers generates the golden section ratio (1: 1.618. . .) to ever more decimal places the higher the Fibonacci numbers.[1]

Figure 15.8 Eden Project Education Resource Centre – the Core (courtesy of Peter Cook/VIEW, Grimshaw Architects)

Its 350 m^2 of photovoltaic cells are, coincidentally, analogous to photosynthesis, and earth ducts supplying either warm or cool air suggest the roots of a tree. Grimshaw teamed up with services engineers Buro Happold to maximize the sustainability credentials of the building such as:

- recycled ground water for toilets
- anaerobic digester producing compost from food waste
- recycled cellulose insulation
- passive cooling except for spaces of high occupancy
- low-energy lighting
- biomass boiler (see Fig. 15.9).

The heart of the sustainability agenda is the biomass boiler. The original intention was to tap into the three 3 MW boilers of the main energy centre. Buro Happold recommended that an alternative would be a biomass boiler of 300 kW capacity; more than enough to cope with the Core's peak demand of 250 kW. It was calculated that such a boiler would operate on average at full load for 10 hours a day delivering about 1100 MWh of heat a year. With a combustion efficiency of 80% this meant a fuel energy input of ~1370 MWh/yr. The fuel mix would consist of:

- woodland residue from 320 ha of managed forests within a 10 km radius
- short rotation coppice willow ~30 ha within a 5 km radius
- miscanthus ~22 ha within a 5 km radius.

The inauguration of the Core coincided with massive rises in the price of gas, which has greatly improved the cost-effectiveness of the biomass boiler. This has been accentuated by the fact that the Eden overall site load is less than 300 kW for over 60% of the year. This meant that the 3 MW boilers were operating well below their peak capacity and therefore

Ventilation Strategies:

Hot Summer Day:

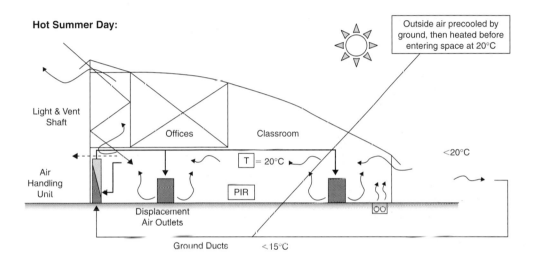

Cool Winter Day:

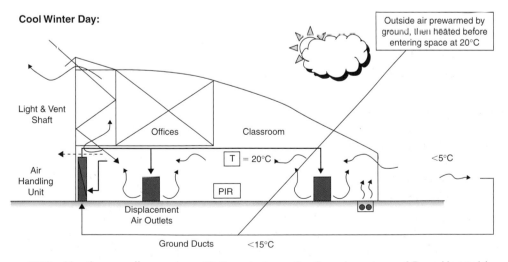

Figure 15.9   Heating, cooling and ventilation strategy, the Core (courtesy of Buro Happold, Services Engineers)

were inefficient. Consequently, integrating the 300 kW boiler into the main system could result in much reduced operating costs (see Chapter 8).

The big environmental benefit is that the biomass boiler saves around 200,000 kg of CO_2 per year.

Overall this is a building which succeeds in achieving an excellent synthesis between function, symbolism, aesthetic quality and a near carbon neutral energy footprint. Congratulations all round.

Council offices, King's Lynn

When the Borough Council of King's Lynn in Norfolk was obliged to consider new accommodation there was a commitment to create a building which was exemplary in both aesthetic and environmental terms. The Borough Council took its obligations under Agenda 21 extremely seriously.

King's Lynn is a tight-knit town with buildings spanning from the twelfth to twenty-first centuries. The new offices occupy a corner site close to a Grade 1 listed church. Jeremy Stacey Architects were commissioned to produce a design which acknowledged the visual 'grain' of the town whilst offering an environmental performance which would place it amongst the leaders in ecological design (see Fig. 15.10).

The fabric of the building achieves well above Regulations standards for thermal efficiency:

	U-values (W/m^{2}K)
Roof	0.13
Walls	0.20
Ground floor	0.16
Windows triple glazed with integral venetian blinds	1.7

Figure 15.10   Borough Council offices, King's Lynn, Norfolk (courtesy of Ecotech)

Careful detailing achieves an air infiltration rate of $5m^3/hr/m^2$ of the building envelope at 50 Pa.

For ventilation the technology chosen was the Termodeck system in which ducts are incorporated into the concrete floor planks (see Chapter 3). One hundred per cent fresh air is mechanically supplied to each room with the corridors used as return air ducts. Condensing boilers provide heat for the air handling system. This unit also ensures that 90% of the heat in exhaust air is recovered. In summer, night-time cooling of the fabric keeps the daytime temperature to within 3°C of the normal set control temperature for refrigeration-based systems. Exposed ceiling soffits provide the radiant cooling. All this means that there is virtually no maintenance burden associated with the ventilation, heating and cooling of the offices. The occupants have additional control over ventilation by being able to open windows.

Solar panels with electrical back-up provide the energy for the hot water system.

The running costs of the offices stand at about one quarter those for a fully air conditioned equivalent which reinforces the axiom that green buildings really do pay.

This is a building which combines excellence of urban design with the level of commitment to ecological imperatives which must become universal if buildings are ever to shed their image as the key drivers of global warming through their associated CO_2 emissions. It also happens to be a well-conceived aesthetic contribution to the fabric of a historic town.

'SkyZed'

Tower blocks are usually regarded as the antithesis of green building. Bill Dunster Architects have tackled this perception head-on with the concept design for a zero energy tower. The argument is that urban densities will have to increase which will make some high-rise development inevitable, therefore the task is to exploit their height and floor plate to make them net sources of power. The tower could form the focal point of a larger low-rise housing complex on the lines of BedZED (see below) and could rise to 35 storeys.

The tower consists of four lobes or 'petals' which direct the wind into a central void containing wind turbines. Wind velocity tests indicate that air flow at the core of the building would be multiplied four-fold by the configuration of petal plan. This would be sufficient to power several vertical axis turbines which would be almost silent. At the same time the floor plates are designed to provide maximum views whilst optimizing daylight (see Fig. 15.11).

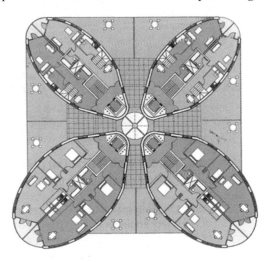

Figure 15.11   SkyZed accommodation lobes which gave rise to the term 'flower tower' (courtesy of Bill Dunster)

Figure 15.12 SkyZed tower and in context (courtesy of Bill Dunster)

On every fourth floor there are triple glazed lobbies linking the petals and providing platforms for viewing the turbines. Additional electricity is provided by PVs on the south-facing façade and south sloping roofs. According to engineers Whitby Bird the combination of low- and high-rise housing would be self-sufficient in electricity (see Fig. 15.12).

To complete its sustainability credentials all grey and black water would be recycled via reed beds located in the shadow of the tower. Much of the construction would employ reclaimed materials: ground granulated blast-furnace slag (ggbs) would be a concrete aggregate whilst reclaimed timber would provide stressed-skin panels.

The commercial viability of the project would be enhanced by the inclusion of work and community spaces on the ground floor. The high density of 115 homes per hectare is the factor which does most for the marketability of the project. That should keep the accountants happy. What would keep the residents happy is the possibility of living and working within the locality of the site whilst enjoying the benefits of ultra-low energy construction.

Figure 15.13   Completed project west elevation

Beddington Zero Energy Development (BedZED)

Though this project featured in the first edition, BedZED has still not been surpassed as a pioneer development. It is not just another low-energy housing scheme, it is a prescription for a social revolution; a prototype of how we should live in the twenty-first century if we are to enjoy a sustainable future. This project was introduced at the foundations stage in *Architecture in a Climate of Change* (pp. 76–78). The scheme now has its first residents and it is appropriate in this volume to consider the completed product (see Fig. 15.13).

It shares many of the objectives of the Malmö development though being on a much smaller scale and so makes an interesting comparison. The main difference is that there is a just one design team led by Bill Dunster Architects who is one of the UK's top evangelists for ecologically sustainable architecture.

To recapitulate, the Innovative Peabody Trust commissioned this development as an ultra-low energy mixed-use scheme for the London Borough of Sutton. It consists of 82 homes with 271 habitable rooms, 2,500 m^2 of space for offices, workspaces, studios, shops and community facilities including a nursery, organic shop and health centre, all constructed on the site of a former sewage works – the ultimate brownfield site. The housing comprises a mix of one- and two-bedroom flats, maisonettes and town houses.

Peabody was able to countenance the additional costs of the environmental provisions on the basis of the income from the offices as well as the homes. Though the Trust is extremely sympathetic to the aims of the scheme, it had to stack up in financial terms.

In every respect this is an integrated and environmentally advanced project. It is a high-density development along the lines recommended by the Rogers Urban Task Force.

It realizes an overall density of 50 dwellings per hectare plus 120 work spaces per hectare. At such a density almost 3 million homes could be provided on brownfield sites with the additional benefit of workspaces for the occupants, radically cutting down on the demand for travel. This density includes the provision of 4000 m^2 of green space including sports facilities.

Figure 15.14   South elevation with work spaces at ground level and roof gardens serving dwellings opposite

Figure 15.15   Masonry wall construction (courtesy of Bill Dunster)

Excluding the sports ground and placing cars beneath the 'village square' the density could be raised to 105 homes and 200 workspaces per hectare.

Some dwellings have ground-level gardens whilst the roofs of the north-facing work spaces serve as gardens for the adjacent homes (see Fig. 15.14).

The energy efficiency of the construction matches anything in the UK or mainland Europe. External wall consist of concrete block inner leaf, 300 mm of rockwool insulation and an outer skin of brick adding up to a U-value of 0.11 W/m^{2}K (see Fig. 15.15).

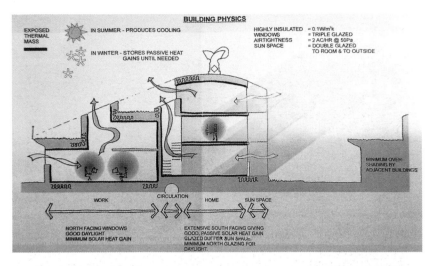

Figure 15.16   Section showing the passive features (courtesy of ARUP and BRE)

Roofs also contain 300 mm of insulation, in this case styrofoam with a U-value of 0.10. Floors containing 300 mm of expanded polystyrene also have a U-value of 0.10. Windows are triple glazed with Low-E glass and argon-filled. They are framed in timber and have a U-value of 1.20. These standards of insulation are a considerable improvement over those required by Part L of the latest Building Regulations in the UK. Masonry external and internal walls and concrete floors provide substantial thermal mass, sustaining warmth in winter and preventing overheating in summer. In traditional construction up to 40% of warmth is lost through air leakage. In the case of BedZED great attention has been paid to maximizing air tightness which is designed to achieve two air changes per hour at 50 pascals.

One of its primary aims was to make the most of recycled materials and the main success in this respect was to obtain high-grade steel from a demolished building as well as timber. The majority of all the materials were sourced within a 35-mile radius.

Materials containing volatile organic compounds (VOCs) have been avoided as part of the strategy to use low-allergy materials.

Ventilation becomes an important issue as better levels of air tightness are achieved. In this case the design team opted for passive natural ventilation with heat recovery driven by roof cowls. A vane mounted on the cowls ensures that they rotate so that incoming air always faces upwind with exhaust air downwind. The heat recovery element captures up to 70% of the heat from the exhaust air.

The energy efficiency drive does not end there. South-facing elevations capitalize on solar gain with windows and their frames accounting for nearly 100% of the wall area. Sun spaces embracing two floors on the south elevation add to the quality of the accommodation (see Figs 15.16 and 15.17).

According to the UK government's method of measuring the energy performance of buildings, the Standard Assessment Procedure for Energy Rating of Dwellings (1998) (SAP), BedZED achieves 150. Until the 2002 revision of the Regulations dwellings were required to achieve around SAP 75. It is predicted that space heating costs will be reduced by 90% against a SAP 75 building. Overall energy demand should be reduced by 60%.

BedZED aims to reduce domestic water consumption by 33%. This is to be achieved by the use of water-saving toilets, dishwashers and washing machines. Toilets normally use 9 litres per flush; regulations now stipulate a 7.5 litre maximum. Here 3.5 litre dual flush toilets are

Figure 15.17   South elevation with PVs integrated into the glazing

provided, producing an estimated saving of 55,000 litres per household per year. Taps are fitted with flow restrictors; showers that rely on gravity replace baths in single bedroom flats. As the scheme uses metered water it is expected that these measures will save a household £48 per year. On average, 18% of a household's water requirements will be met by rainwater stored in large tanks integrated into the foundations.

Foulwater is treated in a sewage treatment plant housed in a greenhouse. It is a biologically based system which uses nutrients in sewage sludge as food for plants. The output from the plant is of a standard equivalent to rainwater and therefore can supplement the stored rainwater to be used to flush toilets.

Household waste normally destined for landfill will be reduced by 80% compared with the average home.

The energy package

The principal energy source for the development is a combined heat and power unit which generates 130 kW of electric power. This is sufficient for the power needs of the scheme. The plant also meets its space heating and domestic hot water requirements via a district heating system served by insulated pipes. The CHP plant is reckoned to be of adequate output due to the high standard of insulation and air tightness and the fact that the peaks and troughs of seasonal and diurnal temperature are flattened by the high thermal mass.

A combustion engine generates the heat and power, producing 350,000 kWh of electricity per year. It is fuelled by a mixture of hydrogen, carbon monoxide and methane produced by the on-sight gasification of wood chips which are the waste product from nearby managed woodlands. The waste would otherwise go to landfill. The plant requires 1100 tonnes per year, which translates to two lorry loads per week. In the future rapid rotation willow coppicing from the adjacent ecology park will supplement the supply of woodland waste. Across London 51,000 tonnes of tree surgery waste is available for gasification. It is worth restating that this is virtually a carbon neutral route to energy since carbon taken up in growth

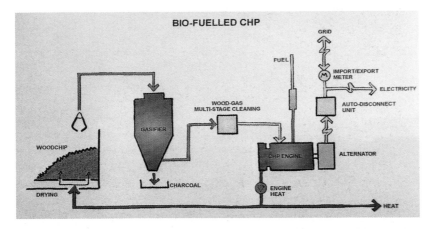

Figure 15.18 Wood chip gasification plant within the development (courtesy of ARUP and BRE)

is returned to the atmosphere. Excess electricity is sold to the National Grid whilst any short-fall in demand is met by the Grid's green tariff electricity. It is predicted that the scheme will be a net exporter to the Grid (see Chapter 8 and Fig. 15.18).

There is a further chapter to the energy story. Figure 15.17 illustrates the inclusion of PVs in the south-glazed elevations of the scheme. They are also sited on southerly facing roofs. Their purpose is to provide a battery charging facility for electric vehicles. How the decision was made to dedicate the PVs to this role is worth recording.

Originally the idea was to use PVs to provide for the electricity needs of the buildings. Evacuated tube solar collectors would provide the heating. It turned out that this arrangement would involve a 70-year payback timescale. If the electricity were to be used to displace the use of fossil fuels in vehicles, taking into account their high taxation burden, the payback time would be about 13 years. So it was calculated that 777 m^2 of high-efficiency monocrystalline PVs would provide a peak output of 109 kW, sufficient for the energy needs of 40 light electric vehicles covering 8500 km per year. It has to be remembered that, in a project like BedZED, the energy used by a conventional car could greatly exceed that used in the dwelling. As a yardstick, a family car travelling 12,000 miles (19,000 km) per year produces almost as much carbon as a family of four living in a typical modern home.

The aim is that the 40 vehicles would provide a pool of cars to be hired by the hour by residents and commercial tenants. Other car pool schemes have indicated that hiring a pool car to cover up to 13,000 km a year could save around £1500 in motoring costs. And that is without factoring in the potential avoided cost of pollution. With congestion charges levied on vehicles using streets in London and soon in other major cities, the exemption of electric vehicles provides an even greater incentive to adopt this technology.

The co-developers Peabody and Bioregional agreed as part of the terms of the planning consent to enter into a Green Travel Plan, which meant a commitment to minimize the residents' environmental impact from travel. On-site work and recreational facilities, together with the electric vehicle pool of 'Zedcars', more than satisfy that commitment.

A diagram produced by Arup summarizes the ecological inventory of the project (see Fig. 15.19).

This development has come about because the right people were able to come together in the right place at the right time. The idea came from Bioregional Development Group, an environmental organization based in Sutton who secured Peabody as the developer. Peabody

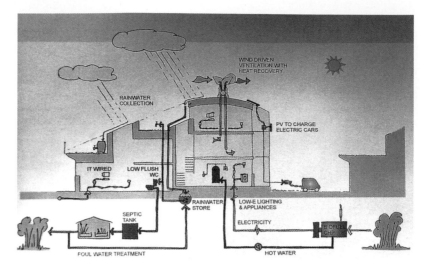

Figure 15.19   The ecological inventory of BedZED (courtesy of ARUP and BRE)

is one of the most enlightened housing associations in Britain. Bill Dunster was engaged on the strength of Hope House, which he designed as an ecologically sound living/working environment and which served as a prototype for BedZED. Chris Twinn of Ove Arup and Partners worked with Bill Dunster when the latter was with Michael Hopkins and Partners so he was a natural choice as adviser on the physics and services of BedZED. The project happened due to a fortuitous conjunction of people committed to the principles of sustainable development. In future, developments of this nature must not rely on the chance collision of the brightest stars in the environmental firmament.

For a more detailed description of this project, refer to 'General Information Report 89, BedZED.[2] The conclusion to be drawn from these case studies is that sustainable design is a holistic activity and demands an integrated approach. Reducing the demand for energy and generating clean energy are two sides of the same coin. Examples have been cited where buildings and transport are organically linked with building integrated renewables providing power for electric cars. BedZED and to some extent Malmö are signposts to new and much more sustainable and agreeable patterns of life. This book has been an attempt to illustrate how the link between buildings and renewable technologies can form a major part of the green revolution which must happen if there is to be any chance of stabilizing atmospheric CO_2 at a level which leaves the planet tolerably inhabitable.

Notes

1.   For a detailed discussion about the relationship between the Fibonacci Series and buildings see *The Dynamics of Delight – Architectural aesthetics*, Peter F. Smith, Routledge 2004
2.   Beddington Zero Energy Development, Sutton, published by BRECSU at BRE, e-mail address: brecsuenq@bre.co.uk

16 Sustainability on a knife edge

Global warming is taking us by surprise. Scientists are regularly having to recalibrate their predictions for impacts in the face of the accelerating evidence of climate change. The most dramatic example of this occurred in 2005. Before this the definitive prognosis for global average temperature rise to 2100 was the IPCC Third Assessment Report of 2001. It estimated that CO_2 emissions were likely to raise average global temperature between 1.4 and 5.8°C.

In January 2005 the results were published of the most extensive study ever conducted on a wide range of climate scenarios. They factored in such things as the extent and rate at which CO_2 abatement was achieved on a world-wide scale and the uncertainties arising from positive feedback. To cope with the enormous computing power needed to manage the 2017 simulations of this programme 90,000 PCs across the world were recruited to use their spare capacity to run the general circulation model adapted from the Met Office Unified Model. The result was a range of 'climate sensitivities', that is, a range of potential temperature rises based on the assumption that CO_2 concentration in the atmosphere would rise to over 500 ppm, or double the pre-industrial level.

The result was a new range of temperature increases from 1.9°C to 11.5°C. The scatter of probabilities formed a bell curve with the highest probability being 3.4°C, though many were much more severe at lower probability. Another multi-PC program is currently under-way to enlist an even greater number of computers.

One of the events which jolted scientists was the breakaway of the Larson B ice shelf off north west Antarctica in 2002 amounting to 3250 square kilometres of floating ice. It will not contribute to sea level rise but, since ice shelves in this region buttress the West Antarctic ice sheet, there is now significantly less to prevent the ice sliding into the sea. In 2005 it was cal-culated that Antarctic glaciers are discharging 110 cubic kilometres to the sea each year.

Greenland is even more dramatic with its two main glaciers adding 120 cubic kilometres annually to the sea. The most recent study (2006) reported in the journal *Science* estimates that, overall, Greenland deposited 224 cubic kilometres into the sea in 2005.[1] In total melt-down the combined effect of the Greenland and West Antarctic ice sheets would be to add 12 metres to the height of the oceans. Also in the last 18 months it has become apparent that mountain glaciers are rapidly contracting. Over the last century the Alps lost 50% of their ice, mostly in the late decades. The Himalayas are losing ice faster than anywhere else on Earth.

In September 2005 it was reported that the whole of the Siberian Sub-Arctic region is melting due to an overall temperature rise of 3°C in 40 years. The Siberian bogs could release 70 million tonnes of methane, a greenhouse gas 23 times more potent than CO_2 described as an ecological landslide undoubtedly linked to global warming.[2]

Despite these signs, the international community is showing little collective will to take emergency action to stop the world crossing one of two critical thresholds, the so-called 'tipping points'. This is to do with concentrations of greenhouse gases in the atmosphere, especially CO_2. At the moment the concentration is around 382 parts per million (ppm) and rising 2–3 ppm per year. The critical threshold is either 400 or 440 ppm depending on who you believe. Beyond this point the melting of ice becomes irreversible and positive feedback enters unknown territory. Unless something remarkable happens we shall cross the tipping point somewhere between 2012 and 2035. It is a sobering thought that when there was no ice on the planet sea level was 120 metres higher than during the last ice age – perhaps 80 m so higher than at present.

The spectre of energy

The second critical threshold advancing inexorably relates to energy. In sharp contrast to the warnings from the climatologists is the optimism of the energy industry based on predictions of unimpeded world economic growth. However, a forecast contained in the International Energy Agency (IEA) *World Energy Outlook* 2004 report suggests that developed countries will increasingly be at the mercy of OPEC (Organisation of Petroleum Exporting Countries). This cartel is set to provide half of the world's supplies of crude oil. The report warns that 'As international trade [in oil] expands, risks will grow of a supply disruption at the critical chokepoints through which oil must flow'. Reliance on fossil fuels will increase over the next two decades with the IEA forecasting that 85% of the increased energy consumption will be met by burning oil, gas or coal. The IEA also estimates that the cost of the new infrastructure to meet the growing demand for oil would be in the region of $16 trillion.

By 2020 the IEA estimates that world energy demand will have risen to 550 EJ (~13,000 mtoe) from about 440 EJ in 2004. Figure 16.1 shows the breakdown of fuels under this projection. By 2030 this will have risen to ~683 EJ (IEA 2005).

Another forecaster is the World Energy Council. Its medium to high growth projection more or less corresponds to the IPCC Business as Usual scenario, extending energy growth to 2100 (see Fig. 16.2). Global consumption in 2004 grew by 4.3%, which is the largest ever annual increase in primary energy consumption. Some, but not all, of the increase was driven by China, which increased its consumption by 15.1%. Over the last three years China's consumption of energy increased by 65% and it now accounts for ~14% of world energy demand. In 2005 it became the world's second largest importer of oil.

There is general agreement that reserves of fossil fuels are finite. Where opinions differ is over the dates at which oil, gas and coal will run out. A timetable produced by the Open University suggests that oil reserves will last about 40 years, gas about 60 years and coal 200 years.[3] The latter could be nearer 100 years as coal is used to compensate for decline in oil and gas.

However, these estimates may be optimistic, depending on probable intervening factors. Based on the IEA forecast of annual oil consumption of 4.46 billion tonnes by 2010, conventional oil reserves will be exhausted by 2040. However, the Agency also predicts that demand will have risen to 5.26 billion tonnes by 2020, which is tenable considering the economic development of China, India, South America and the expected exponential rise in transport. In this

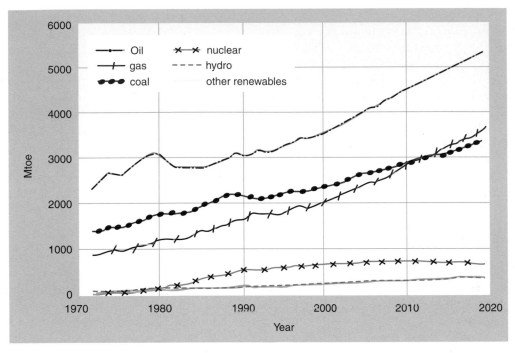

Figure 16.1 International Energy Agency projections to 2020 by fuel (courtesy of IEA)

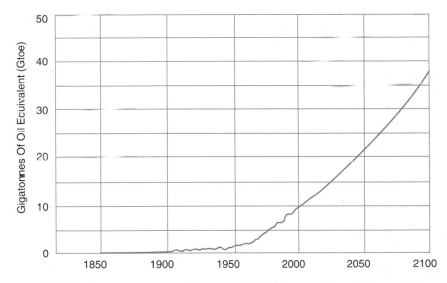

Figure 16.2 Global primary energy use forecast – World Energy Council Scenario based approximately on IPCC Business as Usual scenario. On the basis of the WEC scenario the likely level of primary energy use by 2100 is in the region of 40 Gtoe (gigatonnes of oil equivalent: 1Gtoe = 42 exajoules)

case conventional oil will be used up by 2035.[4] Oil consumption rose by 3.4% in 2004, which represents the fastest rise since 1978. China accounted for more than 33% of the increase.

The second critical threshold may be regarded as the point at which oil production is unable to match rising demand known as 'peak oil'. Colin J. Campbell of the Geneva-based

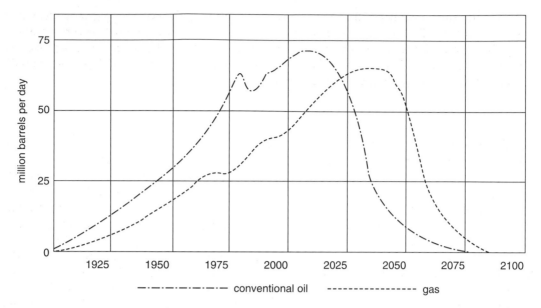

Figure 16.3   Prediction of world production of conventional oil and gas to 2100 based on ASPO

Petroconsultants, a world-renowned expert on the subject, considers that peak oil was reached in 2005. Others put the date nearer to 2010. The difference is insignificant compared with the consequences in the marketplace. Once past the peak oil line price volatility will likely become increasingly severe with serious economic consequences. Already prices are steadily rising, confirming the view that the age of cheap oil is well and truly over. As previously mentioned, the price of US crude is expected to break the $100 a barrel mark in the not-too-distant future.

There will be no escape from the impact of high oil prices such as higher food prices leaving increasing populations facing hunger. Also, there is said to be a direct connection between the price of oil and the rate of unemployment.

In addition there are non-conventional sources of oil extracted from tar sands, shale, bitumen, heavy oil and deep water sources. These impose much higher extraction costs and will only offer a short respite for the market. Figure 16.3 offers a scenario for oil and gas which confirms the peak oil date of ~2005 for conventional oil. Campbell predicts the combination of conventional and non-conventional oil peaking in 2007.

'If production rates fall while demand continues to rise, oil prices are likely to spike or fluctuate wildly raising the prospect of economic chaos . . . and even war as countries fight over what little oil remains'.[3] This is the view of analyst Jeremy Rifkind of the US Foundation of Economic Trends. He continues: 'If we think oil is a problem now, just wait 20 years. It'll be a nightmare'.[4]

Gas

The average of five estimates for gas reserves is around 144 trillion m^3. If annual extraction rates are at around 2.3 trillion m^3, this equates to about 62 years of supply. However, the rate of conversion to gas-fired power generation continues unabated which could make the exhaustion date as soon as 2040. If oil becomes prohibitively expensive due to declining reserves and possible disruption, it may well become cost-effective to convert transport propulsion to fuel cells using hydrogen reformed from natural gas. In this case, reserves could disappear by 2035 or sooner. The world is on course to meet the 2035 prediction with gas consumption increasing by 3.3% in 2004.

Coal

On the world scale coal provides 23% of its energy. Of that, 69% is devoted to generating electricity. Reserves of coal are estimated to be 560 billion tonnes,[4] which would be sufficient for the next 160 years at current rates of extraction. According to the IEA, annual consumption will increase from the present ~2.5 billion tonnes to ~3.95 billion by 2020. This would reduce the life expectancy of coal to 123 years. However, there will probably be a considerable increase in the use of coal to compensate for the gradual demise of oil and gas. Gasification and liquefaction for transport fuel would also make big inroads into reserves. Altogether these could lead to reserves being exhausted well before 2100. In 2004 the world's consumption of coal rose by 6.3% with ~75% of the increase due to China.

The US and Canada plan for over 500 new-coal fired plants which will last 30 years. China is planning to build 300 coal-fired power stations and expects to treble the capacity of its coal-fired plants by 2020. Its coal reserves have a high sulphur content. Over the next 25 years coal-fired plants will emit more CO_2 in their lifetime than the total pollution from coal burning in the last 250 years.

China is rapidly approaching superpower status and by 2040 will have overtaken the USA in economic strength and the west will have to adjust to this, all assuming that climate change has not in the meantime wrought catastrophic social and economic damage throughout the world.

Despite its high carbon intensity, coal is being promoted as a zero carbon fuel for the future. One strategy is to liquefy its CO_2 and bury it in extinct oil wells. Another is to gasify coal to produce methane which would be reformed to produce hydrogen to power fuel cells. A third method of CO_2 sequestration is to capture it from fossil fuel power plants and feed it to bioreactors. These are plastic cylinders containing algae which is converted via sunlight and water into biofuels (see 'From smokestack to gas tank', *New Scientist*, 7 October, 2006, p. 28).

Superficially it might be concluded that the depletion of fossil fuel reserves can only help the transition to renewable technologies. On the basis of the present rate of adoption of renewable energy generation it is highly probable that installed renewable resources will not be nearly sufficient to cope with the economic tensions arising from the increasingly bitter competition for the dwindling reserves of gas and oil. On the other hand, using fossil fuels to exhaustion would increase global temperature by ~13°C leading to catastrophic climate consequences.[5]

At the same time it is an inescapable fact that the majority of cultures are wedded to the idea of economic development. Humans are teleological creatures, that is, programmed to seek and achieve goals. For most individuals and states the goal is increasing wealth and security, especially security of energy. A realistic scenario for the future should take account of this fact despite the protests of those who consider the idea of sustainable development to be the ultimate oxymoron.

It is pointless mapping a future which takes no account of the realities of human nature like the desire at least to maintain a present standard of living and the ability to be in denial about unpalatable predictions. That is why it is logical to assume that world economic growth will

Table 16.1   Progressive rate of increase in carbon neutral energy to 2100

Year	%	Total energy (EJ)	Carbon neutral energy (EJ)
2020	20	11.8 (281 mtoe)	2.36 (56.2 mtoe)
2030	30	13.0 (310 mtoe)	3.9 (93.0 mtoe)
2050	50	15.9 (379 mtoe)	7.95 (189.5 mtoe)
2100	80	26.2 (623 mtoe)	20.96 (498.4 mtoe)

Table 16.2   The pace of renewables uptake assuming 80% by 2050

Year	%	Total energy (EJ)	Carbon neutral energy (EJ)
2020	30	11.8 (281 mtoe)	3.5 (84.3 mtoe)
2030	50	13.0 (310 mtoe)	6.5 (155 mtoe)
2050	80	15.9 (379 mtoe)	12.7 (303 mtoe)
2100	80	26.2 (623 mtoe)	20.96 (498.4 mtoe)

continue until at least to the end of the century. In this case we have to indicate the kind of pressure which will fall on the renewable technologies if catastrophic climate change is to be avoided.

A UK scenario of goals for renewable energy capacity will give an insight into the scale of the problem on the world stage. Assuming a net 1% per year growth in energy demand within 2–3% economic growth and a progressive percentage increase in the ratio of carbon neutral energy to conventional energy the situation that emerges is shown in Table 16.1. This assumes 80% from renewables by 2100.

Starting from the UK energy consumption of 233 mtoe or 8.75 EJ of energy in 2002 and incrementing at a net 1% per year, total energy predictions and renewable energy targets to 2100 would be as Table 16.1.

It is possible that, with the uncertainties now being revealed, the pace of global warming will be significantly faster than that assumed in the above 20–30–50–80 scenario. In that case the rate of contribution by carbon neutral energy might have to be accelerated to achieve 80% by 2050 (Table 16.2).

Since the contribution from carbon neutral sources in 2100 will need to be well over twice the total energy expended in the UK in 2004 the question is: has the UK got the capacity to produce this amount of carbon neutral energy?

Figure 16.4 illustrates the possible spread of renewable technologies that will be needed to meet the 1%/year primary energy growth rate to 2100 under the WEC scenario. Anything above the 1% is achieved through energy efficiency gains.

The distribution of the different technologies in exajoules is:

Bioenergy	3.3
Marine energy	5.0
PV and solar thermal	3.05
Wind	2.05
Hydro	1.0
Heat pumps, Stirling CHP etc	1.0
Coal with CO_2 sequestration	5.56
Total	**20.96 EJ**

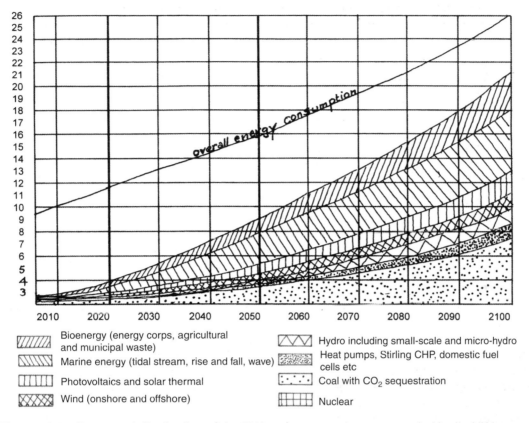

Figure 16.4   Suggested distribution of the 80% carbon neutral energy needed in the UK by 2100 based on the World Energy Council estimate of growth

The above scenario is based on World Energy Council predictions of global growth. It presents an unrealistic and impracticable picture for the UK. Closer to probability is the European Union's estimate for UK total energy growth which predicts it rising from ~240 mtoe or ~9 exa-joules per year to about 270 mtoe or 11.3 exajoules towards the middle of the century. Figure 16.5 depicts the scale of the challenge facing energy suppliers getting close to meeting the UK's declared target of 60% carbon neutral energy by 2050 and 80% by 2100. Under this scenario renewables will be called upon to provide 5 exajoules or 119 mtoe per year by 2050 and 9 exa-joules or 218.2 mtoe by 2100. At the level currently under discussion, nuclear power would make a minor impact, if any, on the final requirement from genuinely renewable technologies.

	EJs	mtoe
Bioenergy	1.5	37.7
Marine energy	2.0	47.6
PV and solar thermal	1.5	37.7
Wind	1.0	23.8
Hydro	0.5	11.9
Heat pumps, Stirling CHP etc	0.5	11.9
Coal with CO_2 sequestration	2.0	47.6
Total	**9.00**	**218.2**

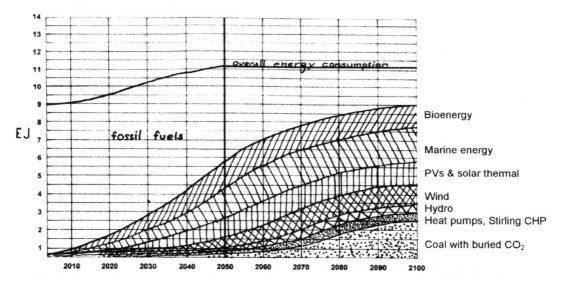

Figure 16.5   Renewables requirement under EU energy consumption scenario for the UK. It is assumed that, after 2050, energy demand will be level and economic growth achieved through energy efficiency gains

To produce this amount of energy will require a generating capacity from renewables of around **162 GW**, which represents 90% of the total energy capacity for the UK, including transport, for 2003.

However, things become less formidable if there is a significant reduction on the demand side. A genuinely sustainable future is only feasible if there is a concerted assault on the CO_2 derived from both the demand and supply sides. Figure 16.6 offers one scenario which assumes that the built environment and transport could realize substantial reductions in demand by 2100, amounting to nearly one-third of total consumption (see Fig. 16.6).

It is challenging but achievable remembering that the UK is especially favoured in the potential to extract energy from its marine resources as indicated in Chapter 11.

In July 2005 the leaders of the three main UK parties entered into an agreement on a strategy to combat terrorism. It was felt to be too important a subject to be undermined by the adversarial politics of Parliament. Earlier, the Government Chief Scientist, Sir David Kind, got universal coverage for his opinion that climate change was an even greater threat than terrorism. Why then can there not be a cross-party consensus on robust strategies to deal with global warming and climate change? Only by removing the risk of electoral penalties will the UK and other democracies be prepared to take the radical actions needed to stabilize CO_2 emissions at a level which will keep the climate within tolerable limits.

There is no doubt that the UK has the natural assets to enable it to be fossil-fuel free in meeting purely its electricity needs by 2030. However, this would require an immediate policy decision by the government to make a quantum leap in its investment in renewable technologies, especially the range of opportunities offered by the tides. This calls for a twin-track strategy.

On the one hand small-scale distributed generation should be vigorously promoted with government subsidies along the lines of the German Renewable Energy Law. Domestic scale heat and power technologies are developing fast and could transform the profile of energy.

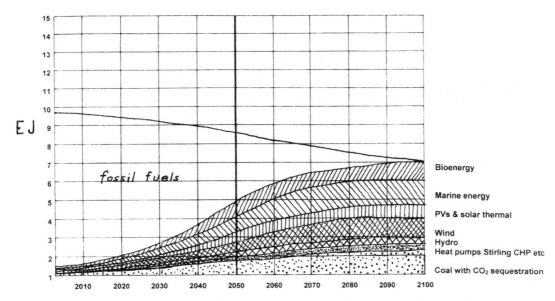

Figure 16.6   A scenario for the profile of renewables with significant demand reduction

On the other hand in parallel there should be development of high-energy intensity or extensive coverage renewables that can deliver base load power to gigawatt level. This mainly concerns tidal power and bioenergy. Neither will take off without substantial government investment. The first step is an integrated energy policy driven by a dedicated government department. The UK government has yet to perceive that energy is at the heart of both its climate change policy and its economic security.

In October 2005 the former UK Energy Minister, Brian Wilson, made a plea for the government to be the driving force behind energy policy rather than leaving the energy future in the hands of the market. He asserted that there must be a new Department of Energy with its own Secretary of State 'who has a clear mandate to promote an agreed policy'. The intention behind this book has been to show that there has never been a time when this has been more urgent. The UK has no more than 5 years in which to change its mindset on energy.

Notes

1.   Report of presentations at the American Association for the Advancement of Science by the Science Editor in St Louis of *The Independent*, 17 February 2006.
2.   See *Global Warming – The complete briefing*, pp. 5–7, John Houghton, Cambridge, 2004
3.   *The Observer*, 4 July 2004
4.   *Vital signs* 2005, p. 56, Worldwatch Publications 2005
5.   'If we don't stop burning oil', *New Scientist*, 18 February 2006, p. 10

Index

Page numbers in *italics* denote figures.